OODGEROO

Kathie Cochrane became interested in the Aborigines in the 1920s at the knee of her grandfather, Edward Armitage, who was adopted as a member of the Wide Bay tribe in the Maryborough region. Known affectionately as "the two Kathies", Kathie Cochrane and Kath Walker (as Oodgeroo was known for most of her life) met as young women in the 1950s, fledgling days of the Aboriginal rights movement in Queensland. They became lifelong friends.

Kathie's previous publications are papers in the field of special education. Before her retirement in 1988 she was senior tutor at the Schonell Education Research Centre, University of Queensland.

Artist Ron Hurley represented Australia at the Fifth Havana Biennale, the international art exhibition, in 1994. He is also director of Queensland Aboriginal Creations, Brisbane.

OODGEROO

KATHIE COCHRANE
with a contribution by Judith Wright

Illustrations by Ron Hurley

University of Queensland Press

First published 1994 by University of Queensland Press
Box 42, St Lucia, Queensland 4067 Australia

© Kathie Cochrane 1994

This book is copyright. Apart from any fair dealing
for the purposes of private study, research, criticism
or review, as permitted under the Copyright Act, no
part may be reproduced by any process without written
permission. Enquiries should be made to the publisher.

Typeset by University of Queensland Press
Printed in Australia by McPherson's Printing Group

Distributed in the USA and Canada by
International Specialized Book Services, Inc.,
5602 N.E. Hassalo Street, Portland, Oregon 97213-3640

Publication of this title was assisted by the Australia
Council, the Federal Government's
arts funding and advisory body

Sponsored by the Queensland Office of Arts
and Cultural Development

Cataloguing in Publication Data
National Libraray of Australia

Cochrane, Kathleen J.
    Oodgeroo

    Bibliography.

    1. Noonuccal, Oodgeroo, 1920- . 2. Women authors,
    Australian—20th century—Biography. [3.] Aborigines,
    Australian—Women—Biography. 4. Australian literature—
    Aboriginal authors—Biography. I. Noonuccal, Oodgeroo,
    1920- . II. Title.

A821.3

ISBN 0 7022 2621 1

*At Oodgeroo's suggestion, this book is dedicated
to the many non-indigenous Australians
who have worked in many different ways
to restore human dignity to the descendants
of the original people of Australia.*

Contents

Publisher's note ix
Preface xi
Acknowledgments xiii

PART ONE LIFE LINES
Beginnings 3
Leaving Home 7
Meetings 25
Relations 43
Protest! 63
Moongalba 87
Acclaim 105
Oodgeroo 127
This Little Now 143

PART TWO POETRY
The Poetry: An Appreciation
by Judith Wright 163

PART THREE SPEECHES
A Stranger in Tasmania 187
Custodians of the Land 200
Beyond Terra Nullius, the Lie 210
Writers of Australia 212

Endnotes 231
List of Copyright Holders 235

Publisher's Note

A month before Oodgeroo died I visited her in hospital. A few hours earlier she had learned that she only had a few months to live. Her courage that day was, as usual, extraordinary.

Kathie Cochrane, her longtime friend, was there with her also, as was Sue Abbey, Oodgeroo's editor at UQP. Oodgeroo was anxious to talk to us about the planned publication of her biography. She wanted to make sure Kathie and UQP had access to particular documents and photographs. I am certain she realised then that she would not live to see the work in print and was entrusting us all with that task.

Her death in September 1993 brought a great sadness to Australia. I first heard the news while driving south, as dawn filtered across vast inland plains. The effect of her passing swelled with each radio news bulletin as Australians responded sorrowfully.

This book, then, is both a promise kept and our tribute to Oodgeroo. It contains not only Kathie Cochrane's very personal account of her friend's life and photographic treasures from private albums, but also the voice of Oodgeroo herself, her poetry.

My last words to her were: "UQP is proud to be the publisher of your life story." That pleased her and it pleases us now to make it a reality.

We believe this warm, intimate portrait honours the indomitable spirit and wisdom of Oodgeroo of the tribe Noonuccal.

Laurie Muller
Publisher and friend

Preface

The first intimation I had that Oodgeroo really wanted me to write the story of her life came one day when we met the water-taxi that had just brought her over from Stradbroke Island. We settled ourselves into our car and as we started for Brisbane, she plonked some manila folders into my lap. "Vivian's notes," she said. "They might help you if you write my biography."

Several people had attempted her biography, most recently her son Vivian, whose untimely death was a huge sorrow to her. On a previous visit she had said "I don't suppose anyone will write my biography now".

"I wonder if I could have a go," I said in a quite uncertain voice, having absolutely no conviction that it was a task I could seriously undertake.

Now that she evidently wanted me to tackle the project, I decided to do my best. After all, she had been my friend for thirty-five years. In the early days of the movement for Aboriginal advancement we had worked together closely and harmoniously. I had developed an enormous respect for her many abilities. If this was a good reason for me to take on the task of telling the story of her life, it did not make it easy.

It is difficult to write a book about a gifted person, and even more so when the person's gifts are multi-faceted. Oodgeroo was blessed with literary and artistic talent but she was also an arresting speaker, an inspired teacher and a visionary. Her vision was for a world in which all people are equal and full of the milk of human kindness, enriched by knowledge of the past and belief in the future.

We worked together closely in the early days of the Aboriginal advancement movement. I knew about her deep desire to express her feelings in poetry—and her achievements as a poet have been widely recognised—but I am no literary critic. My cry for help to her great friend, poet Judith Wright, was answered most generously in the form of a literary appreciation of Oodgeroo's work. For this I am extremely grateful.

Oodgeroo and I grew old together. She was 72 and I was 70 when my husband and I took her to be admitted to the Greenslopes Repatriation Hospital in Brisbane early in August 1993. Five weeks later she was dead. I am just now beginning to recover from her loss, and to feel that it was a privilege for my husband and me to spend time with her in those last weeks. If my book helps people to understand the great contribution that her life has made to the lives of us all it will have been worth the toil. And her poetry is always there.

A note on the spelling of Noonuccal In 1988 Oodgeroo proclaimed herself Oodgeroo of the Noonuccal tribe. Earlier she had sometimes written the word as Noonuckle, which gives an unambiguous representation of the pronunciation of the name current among her people today. More recently, Aborigines on Stradbroke Island have favoured the form Nunukul, but I have retained the Noonuccal spelling because it is the most widely used and has attained public prominence. It is quite common for Aboriginal words to be spelled in different ways in English because of the obvious difficulties of transcribing oral languages.

Acknowledgments

The Fryer Memorial Library at the University of Queensland—a repository of Australian literature, manuscripts, historical documents and personal collections—became a familiar workplace. I am particularly beholden to Margaret O'Hagan, the Fryer Librarian, for facilitating my access to the Kath Walker Collection. I also thank the audio-visual services section of the University of Queensland Library for making available relevant films and videotapes.

There are many to thank for their willing assistance: my husband Bob Cochrane, who typed draft upon draft and gave me assistance and great encouragement at all times; Alastair Campbell, who lent me many old newsletters, reports and other documents concerning the Aboriginal rights movement; and Barrie Pittock also for the loan of important documents. Then there is Elsie Gibson, who allowed me to visit her and go through her impressive collection of newsletters and press clippings; Barbara Poulter, who lent me tapes of Kath addressing students at Moongalba; John Collins, her very dear friend who, as a publisher, was very involved with Oodgeroo's work; and Patricia Walker who supplied wonderful family photographs.

I frequently asked Oodgeroo for details about her various involvements, and she often answered with: "Ring up so-and-so." As a result, I have had many conversations with people who responded most willingly when they understood why I was seeking the information. So I thank Malcolm Blow, Rhonda Craven, Lucy Pettit, Ian Gaillard, Keith Gasteen, Ann Derham, Julianne Schwenke, Graham Bungate, Kevin Power and Richard Hunter.

The staff who work at the North Stradbroke Island Aboriginal and Islander Housing Co-operative Society are acknowledged with gratitude, particularly Dr Wendy Page and Nurse Mary Martin, for bringing me up to date with the many projects Oodgeroo initiated on her beloved Minjerribah.

Oodgeroo's own contribution was vital, her critical comment crucial. It is a source of great satisfaction to me that she had approved of the way I told her story and that it had already been accepted for publication before she died. Thus she knew that the story of her life, as she saw it, would survive.

Part One Life Lines

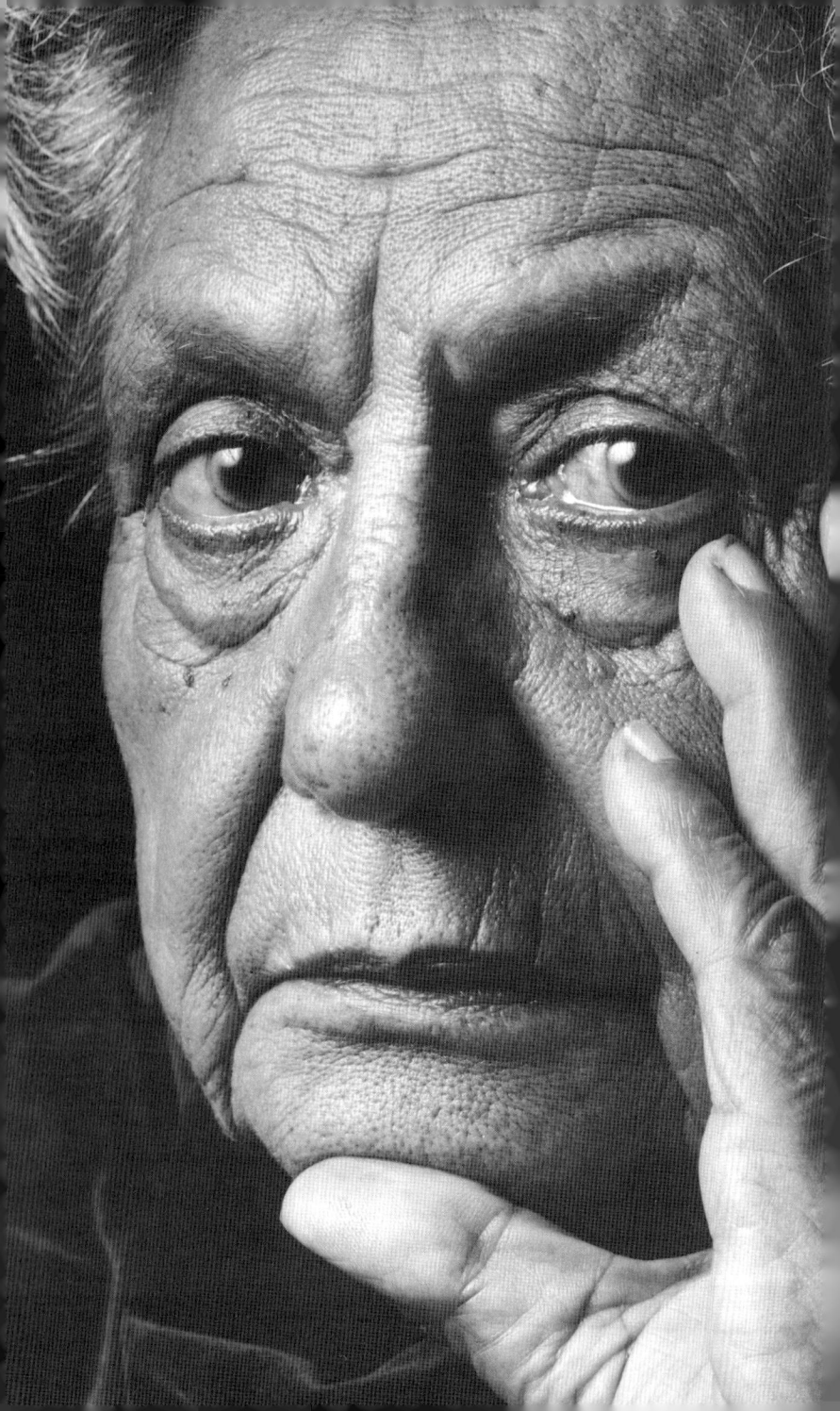

Beginnings

Stradbroke Island is one of the beautiful islands that form part of the Great Sandy Region of southeast Queensland. The Noonuccal people inhabited this island for countless generations. They called it Minjerribah. On 3 November 1920, the newest Noonuccal descendant had just been born.

I arrived about a week before expected, at the home of white friends where there was a wedding in progress; and the little black baby stole the show from the star performer, the bride. They named me Kathleen Jean Mary Ruska.[1]

Since the late 1800s it had been Queensland government policy to gather up Aborigines from various tribes and relocate them in reserves or on church-run missions; it was an effective way of crushing the spirit of a people. Attempts to establish a mission on Stradbroke Island to control the Noonuccal inhabitants, however, had not succeeded. So Kath Ruska grew up with five siblings in the home established by her parents. Stories about the failed mission were told to her by older members of the Noonuccal tribe, but Kath had never experienced the heavy, paternalistic hand of mission rule. She grew up with a strong sense of her Aboriginal identity and the determination to fight for the rights of all her people.

Unfortunately, too few mainland Aborigines had escaped the government's authoritarian net for a civil rights movement to evolve among themselves. So, perhaps inevitably, it fell to non-Aboriginal sympathisers to initiate the movement on their behalf. It was an elderly white woman who first stirred the pot in Queensland, Ada Bromham, a staunch member of the Women's Christian Temperance Union who espoused all causes that might lead to better living standards for the socially disadvantaged. Enthusiastic about advancing the civil rights of indigenous Australians, she was appointed by the Women's Christian

Temperance Union as their Superintendent of Native Races. In this role she became concerned that Queensland, with its relatively large Aboriginal population, would not be represented in Adelaide at a national conference on Aboriginal welfare set down for February 1958. The convenors of the conference were Aboriginal welfare groups in Victoria and South Australia.

On 18 January 1958 she sent letters to any organisation she could discover which had professed an interest in the welfare of Aboriginal Australians. One recipient was the Brisbane Western Suburbs Branch of the United Nations Association. She knew that this group was working on a booklet about the history and current living conditions of Queensland's Aborigines and Torres Strait Islanders.

Its publication later the same year was a milestone in Queensland in that for the first time information on the subject was accessible to a population that had been kept in the dark for so long. Alastair Campbell carried most of the burden of the project, and his co-writers shared his keen and sympathetic interest in Aboriginal welfare: John Keats, Lilian Cameron, Barbara Poulter, and Max Poulter. The booklet, *The Aborigines and Torres Islanders of Queensland*, was enthusiastically received and soon reprinted.[2]

In her letter Ada Bromham asked representatives to attend a conference on Tuesday 28 January at 7.45 p.m. in the YMCA Building, Edward Street, Brisbane. Some thirty-five people turned up, all variously committed to Aboriginal rights and not one of them remotely Aboriginal. The meeting decided to form a Queensland Council for the Advancement of Aborigines and Torres Strait Islanders. Alastair Campbell agreed to take the chair and a provisional committee of ten was elected.

Alastair Campbell played a signal role in the genesis of Aboriginal rights movements in Queensland. A distinguished physician and specialist in chest diseases, he came to Queensland from Victoria in 1955 as director of specialist services in the Commonwealth Repatriation Department. He brought with him a keen interest in civil liberties and the rights of underprivileged people. His work on the UN Association's booklet deepened his involvement; he became increasingly concerned with the inequalities and inhumane treatments meted out to Aboriginal and Islander people under the sanction of Queensland laws.[3]

The fledgling council needed Aboriginal representation, he said. Perhaps my husband Bob and I might drive around areas where Aboriginal families lived, get talking to some people and see if we could interest them in it. We agreed to his suggestion and spent several weekend afternoons boldly knocking on doors.

Almost always it was the woman of the household, wife/mother, who welcomed us, listened politely and then informed us that the person we really must see was Kath Walker. It eventually became clear to us that our intrusive approaches were inappropriate for recruiting Aborigines into a civil rights movement initiated by white Australians. But perhaps, none the less, we had better visit this Kath Walker.

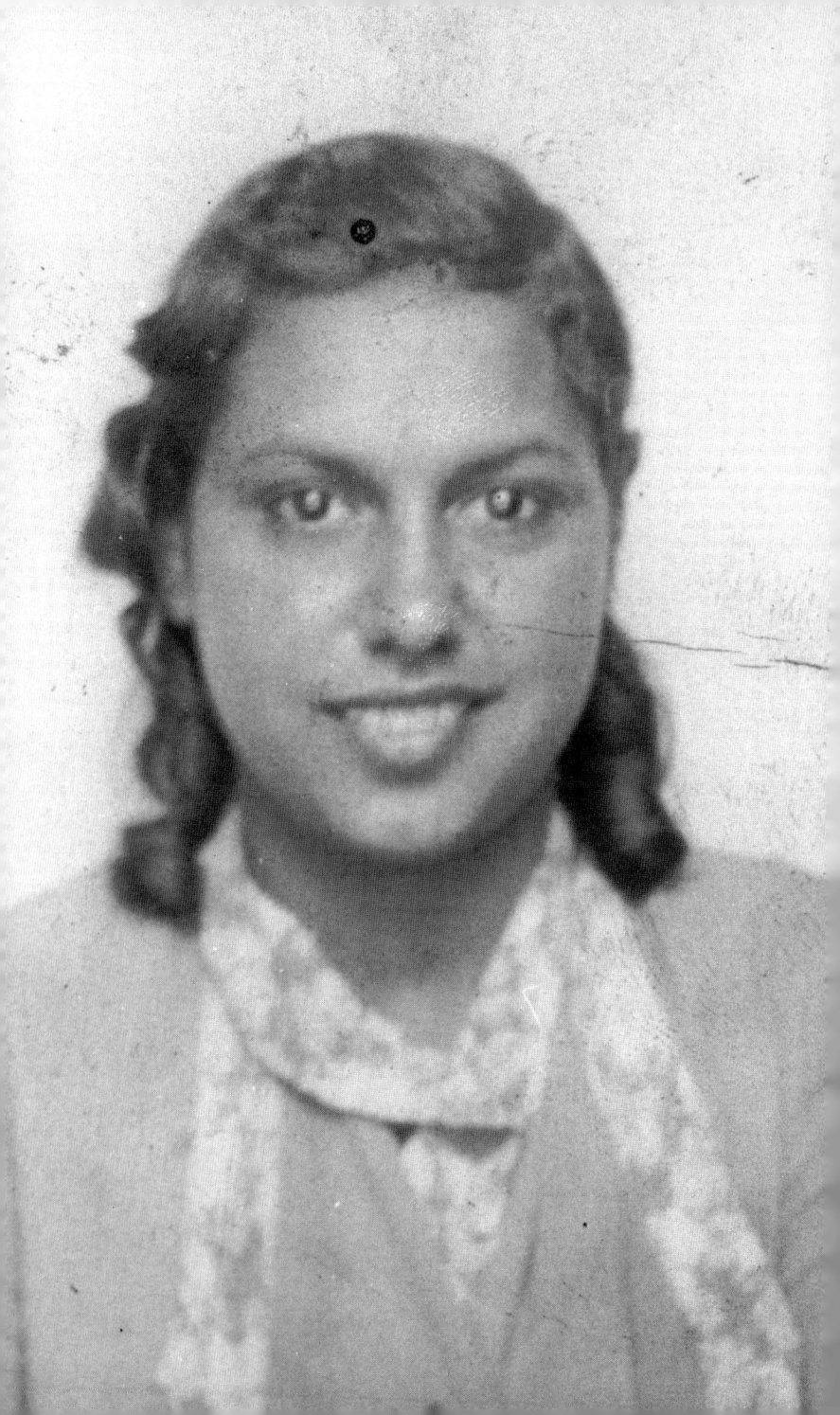

Leaving Home

Back in 1933, on Friday, 15 December, the Dunwich State School on North Stradbroke Island broke up for the Christmas holidays. One of the children coming out of the playground was Kathleen Ruska, a small, slim Aboriginal child who had just turned thirteen. Her formal education was over. She was now considered fit to be put to work, as were most Aboriginal boys and girls at the end of primary schooling and also many white children from poorer families.

Kath was luckier than many of her Aboriginal contemporaries in Queensland, who spent most of their childhood in dormitories. They were fed, clothed and "educated" within a restrictive, authoritarian system; and when a girl reached the age of fourteen, she was assigned to domestic work, usually on a rural property. Kath, however, had been free. Her parents, too, lived a free life in their home at Dunwich, along with her older brothers and sisters Eric, Eddie, Florrie and Lucy, and her younger sister Vivian.

As it happened, she did become a domestic servant. By 1933 the Depression had reached into almost every home in Australia. Ted and Lucy Ruska, her parents, were struggling to maintain their modest lifestyle. They had been able to help their daughter Lucy to enter the nursing profession, but by the time Kath left school there seemed no alternative but live-in domestic service. It was by no means an unusual occupation for young women, black and white alike, in those straitened times.

Her first live-in position was with the family of Herbert McAllister at Coorparoo in Brisbane. She was paid two and sixpence per week in addition to board and lodging. During the next ten years she worked for a number of professional families. The highest weekly wage she earned was thirteen and sixpence; most white domestic servants at the same time were being paid between fifteen shillings and one pound.

Cookalingee
For Elsie Lewis

Cookalingee, now all day
Station cook in white man's way,
Dressed and fed, provided for,
Sees outside her kitchen door
Ragged band of her own race,
Hungry nomads, black of face.
Never begging, they stand by,
Silent, waiting, wild and shy,
For they know that in their need
Cookalingee gives them feed.
Peeping in, their deep dark eyes
Stare at stove with wide surprise,
Pots and pans and kitchen-ware,
All the white-man wonders there.

Cookalingee, lubra still
Spite of white-man station drill,
Knows the tribal laws of old:
"Share with others what you hold";
Hears the age-old racial call:
"What we have belongs to all."
Now she gives with generous hand
White man tucker to that band,
Full tin plate and pannikin
To each hunter, child and gin.
Joyful, on the ground they sit,
With only hands for eating it.
Then upon their way they fare,
Bellies full and no more care.
Cookalingee, lubra still
Feels her dark eyes softly fill,
Watching as they go content,
Natural as nature meant.
And for all her place and pay
Is she happy now as they?

Wistfully she muses on
Something bartered, something gone.
Songs of old remembered days,
The walkabout, the old free ways.
Blessed with everything she prized,
Trained and safe and civilised,
Much she has that they have not,
But is hers the happier lot?

Lonely in her paradise
Cookalingee sits and cries.

Kath often wished she could have been a nurse's aid, like Lucy. When Australia declared war on Germany in September 1939 the Red Cross organised first-aid classes for women. Kath was then working for a household in Ashgrove and she decided to attend the classes in her own time. It was not a comfortable experience. She was ignored by the middle-class white women in the group and the woman she worked for became furious when she found first-aid literature in Kath's bedroom. "You're wasting your time with that," she said. "You can't even understand the language." Kath asked why she shouldn't try to learn all about first aid. "Because, my dear, I happen to be a member of the Red Cross myself and it will be very embarrassing to me if my friends find out that you, my servant, are a member."

There was no conscription for overseas service during the early part of the war, but able-bodied young men were called up for training in the Militia unless their occupations were considered of more importance to the national interest.

Aboriginal men were exempted from call-up because they were not classed as Australian citizens, but they were free to enlist as volunteers if they chose. Kath's brothers Eddie and Eric enlisted in the AIF at the beginning of the war. Both ended their war service in Changi, and both survived, though Eddie lost a leg. In 1941 Kath, nearly twenty-one, decided to enlist in the Australian Women's Army Service (AWAS). She hoped the army would give her some training in new skills so she could escape from the inevitability and the drudgery of domestic work.

When she was summoned to Victoria Barracks for an interview, a female captain warned her that she might experience some racial prejudice in the service. Kath replied that she could see no difference between a racist in uniform and a racist in civvies. As it happened, the advice was unnecessary as Kath was to experience no discrimination in the army.

Bruce Walker and Kath Ruska married in West End, Brisbane, in 1942. The bride's short dress was typical of wartime weddings when clothing materials were rationed.

After a stint of basic training at Yeronga she was sent to Chermside to do a crash course in switchboard operation. The tent barracks were in the middle of scrub, now the site of the Chermside shopping centre. Kath never forgot her tent mates, Eris Valentine and Thora Travis. They gave her her first taste of what it was like to live day in day out in close contact with white people who didn't even notice the colour of her skin. Eris was an ingenious deviser of practical jokes and she frequently enlisted the help of Kath and Thora in carrying them out. Neighbours in nearby tents who were the victims of these pranks dubbed them "the three musketeers".

Kath quickly learned the switchboard operation. She was promoted to corporal and put in charge of training beginners; later she was relocated to the AWAS pay office. Leave for longer than one night was seldom granted to AWAS personnel but, when it was, Kath visited her parents at Dunwich.

Across Moreton Bay North Stradbroke Island had been turned into a fortress. The island was intended to be a buffer zone for Brisbane in case the Japanese broke through the defences to the north. If Brisbane were attacked from the air, Stradbroke would be a medical base; the army was then in the process of transporting medical and food supplies across the bay on the *Otter*. Kath's parents threw open their home to the soldiers who were lining forty kilometres of ocean beach with sand-bagged gun emplacements and trenches.

Bruce Raymond Walker was an old playmate of Kath's. A descendant of the Logan and Albert River tribes nearby on the mainland, he had relations on the island at Dunwich and often visited them as a child. When the friends met again in Brisbane, they fell in love and were married at the Methodist church in West End in 1942. They found a house at 19 Myrtle Street, Buranda, and obtained a loan from a friend, a Mr Beardmore, who had great sympathy for Aboriginal people. They

paid off the loan and so came to own their own house – this was most unusual for an Aboriginal couple in those days.

Bruce also contributed to the war effort. He had been trained as a welder and was engaged on building the Liberty ships at the Kangaroo Point shipyard. These American-designed cargo ships were custom-made for the fast transport of supplies needed for the Allied war effort, and Australia was helping to produce them in the large numbers required.

Since enlisting in AWAS Kath had developed severe middle ear infection and inflammation of the gums, disorders which would not respond to the medications then available. Towards the end of 1943 she was invalided out of AWAS. The ear infection caused a permanent, moderate hearing loss and the gingivitis brought about the loss of all her teeth when she was in her mid-forties.

Her immediate action on leaving the army was to enrol in a shorthand and typing course at the Brisbane Commercial College. With her newly acquired skills she found a job with Dandy Bacon at Murarrie.

Bruce was a bantam-weight boxer and Kath was keen on many sports, including tennis, swimming and softball. They joined the City Pastime Club at West End, where Kath met Ruby Robinson, the women's sport reporter on the *Courier-Mail*. Through playing cricko Kath recognised an opportunity to use the team spirit of sport to bring young Aboriginal women together. She began the Brisbane All-Blacks, a black women's cricko team, cricko being a game played by women which was based on cricket. However, the All-Blacks soon changed games and played vigoro.

Kath was a champion cricko player, an excellent left-hand slow bowler. A member of the Wyworries in the forties and fifties, she twice played for Queensland. Photo taken at Moore Park, Sydney.

LEAVING HOME • 15

ABOVE: At the crease

RIGHT: Receiving the trophy for highest scorer of the match

16 • OODGEROO

Organising matches was difficult because bus companies were reluctant to lease vehicles to the team. Some members became dispirited and dropped out, and eventually Kath gave up and joined a cricko team called the Wyworries. She and her sister Lucy and Lucy's daughter Judy played with the team for many years. Captained by Phyllis Manson, a devoted and energetic sportswoman and a good friend to Kath, the team won the premiership eleven years running. Phyllis recently recalled how youthful Kath looked at the age of thirty: on her way to a match one day in 1950, she was mistakenly charged the child's busfare of one penny.

Bruce and Kath also liked dancing. They knew Aborigines were not "allowed" at many dance halls but they found they were welcome at the Russian Orthodox church hall at Woolloongabba. They told their friends. One night a large group of Aboriginal dance enthusiasts turned up. This frightened the white people, who stopped coming, and soon the hall was closed to all dancers. Kath's concern at this type of fear and prejudice shown by white people soon led her into a more politically active role.

Part of the Walkers' weekly routine was Kath's visit to the butcher on Friday evenings to buy the weekend meat. In those pre-plastic days, newspapers were routinely recycled as wrapping for groceries, meat, fish and chips and so on, outside a layer of plain paper. It was strange but true that people had a particular fascination for reading these sheets of newsprint. Fortuitously, one day in 1944 Kath and Bruce came across a letter to the editor which complained about a store in Bundaberg that displayed a sign in the window saying, "We serve Whites only". Impressed that the paper had published the letter, they looked at it more carefully. It was the *Guardian*, the Communist Party of Australia's weekly tabloid.

Kath decided to follow the matter up and rang the local Communist Party office. She asked about the letter and inquired about their policies with regard to Aboriginal people. They answered her by citing Article 1 of the International Declaration of Human Rights, which states: "All human beings are born free and equal in dignity and rights...and should act towards one another in a spirit of brotherhood."

The party flew her to Bundaberg where they planned a demonstration in front of the store with the racist sign. They had also contacted a local Aboriginal war veteran who had won medals for bravery in the First World War. In full uniform he accompanied a couple of comrades into the store. The whites pretended to be browsing, leaving the Aborigine the only customer ready to be served. This forced the shop assistant to say, "We don't serve blacks here." Party members picketed the store, and the sign was soon removed. The veteran digger borrowed money from the white comrades and went back in to buy a shirt – the first time he had ever shopped there.

Kath and Bruce became interested in the Communist Party. They attended party classes and read Communist literature. However, the Bundaberg incident was the only example of direct action against discrimination that they witnessed; and Kath resented white comrades' wanting to write her speeches against racial discrimination. She never needed anyone to write her speeches for her!

However, as her friend John Collins has observed, one of the reasons for Kath's linguistic, political and strategic skills was that she had learned a great deal from her Communist comrades of the fifties.

> This beguilingly small person, who was larger than lifesize, often brutally frank and as lively as quicksilver and teller of a thousand stories, readily acknowledged her debt to the one political party that didn't have White Australia as a policy plank, the Communist Party of Australia.[1]

In later years Kath tested the waters of other political parties and found them, likewise, disappointing.

Since the fall of Singapore in February 1942, the Ruska family had heard nothing of Eddie and Eric. They believed, without any direct evidence, that their boys had both been captured and taken to Changi. With the end of the war came news that the survivors of the horror camp had been released. Ted and Lucy stayed glued to their radio but cause for hope came in a letter. A ham radio operator in Western Australia had picked up a message from an Eric Ruska, who had asked anyone listening to contact his mother and father and tell them he was alive and would get in touch later.

When Eric did get in touch he told his relieved parents that both he and Eddie had survived the Changi ordeal, but that Eddie had lost a leg. Eric came home soon afterwards, a walking skeleton. He had lost track of Eddie. In desperation Ted wrote to the Minister of Defence, who replied that Eddie had been located in a Sydney repatriation hospital. He had said he didn't want to see his family because he felt too bitter about the loss of his leg. Before the war Eddie had been a promising athlete, an especially fine runner.

After some time it was Kath whom Eddie felt able to contact. He came to stay with her at Myrtle Street for a number of weeks and as a token of his gratitude he had the phone service connected for her. He was deeply disturbed by the Changi experience and the loss of his leg. He sat in the

In Malaya during the war, Eddie Ruska added his photo and Kath's to this personalised banknote souvenir and sent it home to her only days before his capture during the fall of Singapore and his ordeal at Changi.

*"What can I tell you,
son of mine?"*
Denis Bruce Walker,
born December 1946

house constantly stroking and caressing a leg that was not there. At night Kath and Bruce were wakened by his terrible screaming and shouting in a language that sounded like Japanese. In the mornings Kath asked Eddie how he had slept. "Like a top," he would reply.

Help for the disabled in post-war Australia was negligible. There were no counselling services outside hospitals and the general community was far from attuned to the needs of the physically disabled. Kath was shocked at the way people ignored Eddie when he fell over in a bus or was knocked over in the street, and she wondered if a black man with a leg missing was perhaps especially invisible.

At about the same time Kath persuaded Bruce to give up boxing; the violence of the sport had become increasingly distasteful to her. Bruce had protested: "The only place you can legally hit a dugai [white man] is in the ring," which did nothing to increase Kath's regard for the sport. After many arguments he gave in to her urging and promised to stop when he began losing.

His retirement, after he had won forty-two out of forty-five bouts, was, for him, a psychological disaster: he had grown addicted to the admiration and applause of the fight crowd. He took a job as a "wharfie" but, not being the centre of any special attention, became restless and moody and blamed Kath for his unhappiness. He took to wandering up and down the coast from Rockhampton to Sydney, searching for his old associates of the ring and looking in the pubs for former fans. While he was away Kath's first son, Denis Bruce, was born in December 1946. The couple had virtually separated by this time, but Bruce occasionally dropped in at the house. He was genuinely fond of the little boy – and Denis adored his father. Unfortunately the infrequent visits became more and more unpleasant as Bruce turned up drunk and abused Kath verbally and, sometimes, physically. He ceased to contribute to the financial upkeep of the household.

Kath realised that she had to make her way alone. She began taking in laundry to supplement her income from Dandy Bacon. Even in this she experienced racist attitudes: some people, arriving with their clothes baskets, chose not to leave them when they saw that she was black.

As a single parent, Kath found the responsibilities particularly heavy because she was black and her child was black. Soon after Denis started school a letter came from the head teacher asking her to come to the school. It seemed that Denis and three other boys in Grade One had been caught pulling down the girls' pants. The head teacher suggested that Denis be shifted to another school. Kath then enquired about what had happened to the other boys, all of whom were white, and the principal admitted that she had made no complaint to their parents, had not even reported the matter to them. Nevertheless this incident, and other evidence of mischievous, even dangerous, behaviour that greeted her when she returned home from work at about 6 p.m. each evening, convinced Kath that she could no longer keep her job at Dandy Bacon.

With great reluctance she looked at advertisements for domestic help in nearby suburbs. It was her good fortune, as events turned out, that a well-known Brisbane family, the Cilentos, were seeking such help. Kath obtained the position and felt an immediate rapport with the family; a long and friendly relationship began to develop. Both parents were doctors: Raphael (later Sir Raphael) was professor of Tropical Medicine at the University of Queensland; and Phyllis championed new techniques of natural childbirth and was an early advocate of augmenting infant feeding with vitamin-rich fruits and cereals. The couple had a family of highly talented, rather unconventional children, among them the youngest daughter Diane, who became an actor.

Phyllis Cilento's aged mother lived with the family; she had become temperamentally difficult but Kath seemed to have a special ability to cope with her, for which the family was grateful. She was accepted as a valuable addition to the family and the younger Cilentos sometimes visited her at Myrtle Street. She herself was greatly enriched by her daily contact with a family where intelligent conversation, artistic endeavour and dramatic activities were part of everyday life. She was encouraged to try her hand at sculpting and painting; perhaps her association with the Cilentos helped her to recognise her desire to write poetry.

During this time, Kath conceived another child; Raphael Cilento junior was the father. Young Raff never publicly acknowledged his paternity of Vivian, who was born in February 1953. Bruce still visited very occasionally, but he ignored the child who so obviously was not his.

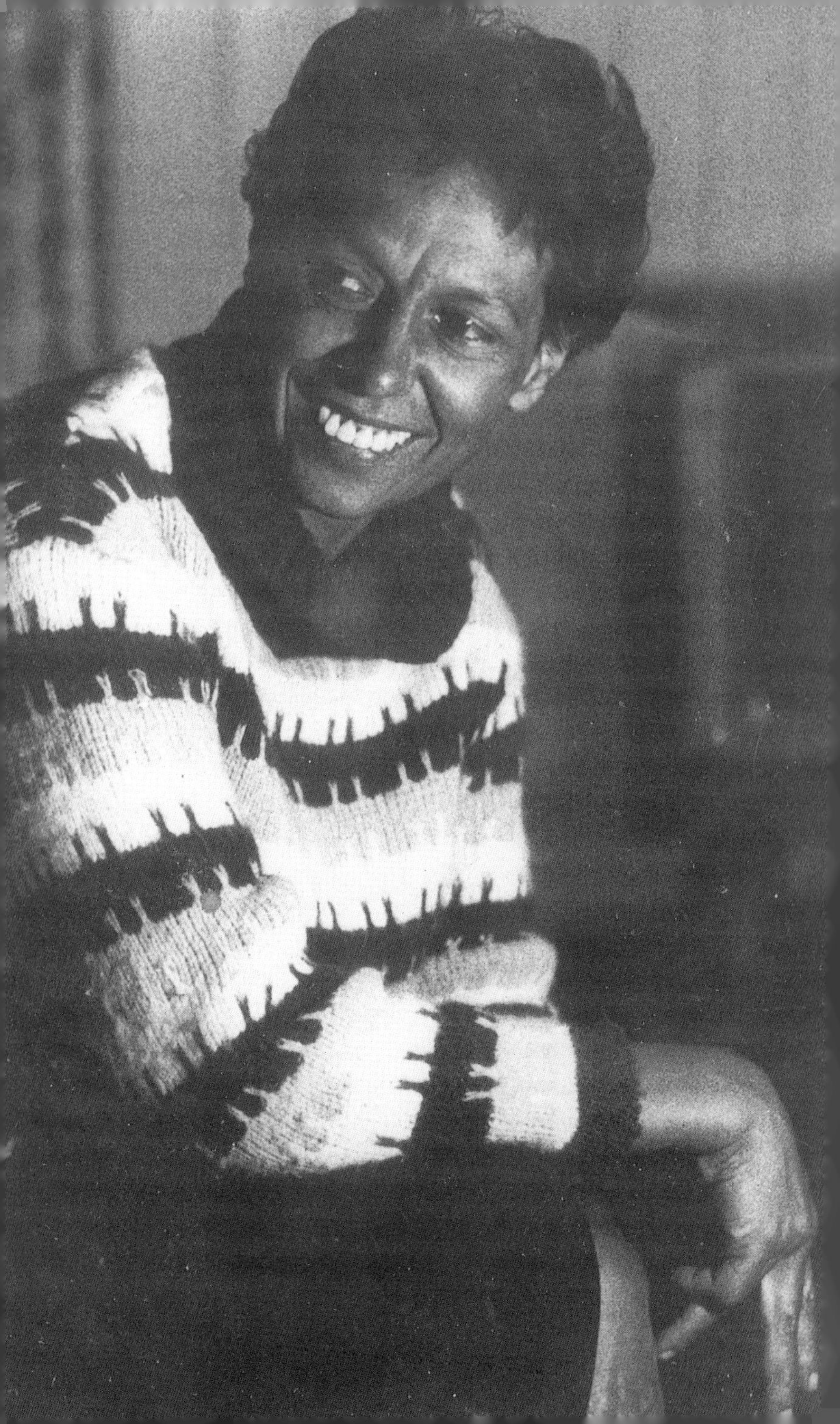

Meetings

One Saturday afternoon in 1958 Bob and I drove across to Myrtle Street. We felt apprehensive. So many of the Aboriginal families we had visited had mentioned that Kath Walker might be interested in a movement for Aboriginal rights, but would she be, or would we be politely turned down again? As I haltingly began the usual, fairly long-winded explanation for our visit, Kath interrupted with "Come on in". We went along a small passage to her sitting-room.

She soon understood why we had come. We had only to explain to her that the Queensland Council had been formed in January and that a Federal Council had followed from the Adelaide conference in February, and she was immediately interested. But she had something to say, too, and I suddenly knew that there was no reason for our nervousness. This unusual woman had put us completely at our ease.

"It's funny," she said, "I've just finished writing a short story about a returned serviceman – an Aborigine – who was treated as an equal by his white mates in the army. But what do you think happened to him after he was demobbed?"

"You write?" I interrupted. "You write stories?"

"Actually I'm more interested in writing poetry," she said, "but I have just written this story. Would you like to hear it?" She read us a story about the disillusionment and disappointment of a man who had been on equal terms with his army mates, but who went to a city pub with some of them just after his discharge and was served with noticeable reluctance. When he returned to his hometown in the country he encountered the same discrimination he had previously known.

It was an impressive story and Bob and I asked if she would consider getting it published. She belonged to the Realist Writers, she told us, a group that met regularly to read and criticise each other's work and had ideas about where to look for a publisher.

Studio photo of Kath, Vivian and Denis, taken in about 1957

Bob and I could not have guessed that a warm, lifelong friendship would grow out of that extraordinary afternoon; and neither could Kath have realised that she had just been recruited into a movement for Aboriginal rights whose cause she was to champion for the rest of her days.

Kath agreed to attend meetings of the Queensland Council for the Advancement of Aborigines and Torres Strait Islanders (QCAATSI). I had explained that the Council had been formed on the initiative of Ada Bromham because of the pending Adelaide conference which aimed to set up a federal advancement movement. I told her that Ada had approached various people, including Alastair Campbell and Alec McDonald, secretary of the Queensland Trades and Labor Council. Alec's involvement was to have the unfortunate effect of arming those who were opposed to changing the status quo with a weapon to brand the whole attempt as Communist inspired, for Alec was well known as a member of the Communist Party.

Ada attended the Adelaide conference in February, at which the Federal Council for Aboriginal Advancement (FCAA) was set up and she was elected vice-president. (The name was later changed to FCAATSI, at the insistence of the Queensland Council, to include Torres Strait Islanders.) From Adelaide Ada went on to Perth to help nurse her sister who had become ill, and she never returned to live in Brisbane. It says something for her determination and energy that, in less than two months, she had galvanised into action many people from diverse backgrounds in the interests of Aboriginal rights. Had she returned to Brisbane, many of the troubles that lay ahead for the Queensland Council might have been avoided.

From its earliest days, QCAATSI was beset by hostility, both overt and covert, from people whose interests were vested in denying Aborigines and Islanders their civil rights. The *Queensland Aborigines Preservation and Protection Acts, 1939–1946* were iniquitous laws that gave the government a mandate for total authoritarian control over the Aboriginal settlements at Cherbourg, Woorabinda, Mappoon, Bamaga and other places. (Hereafter the legislation is referred to as the Queensland Acts.) The Department of Native Affairs (DNA) supervised the movement of Aboriginal people between settlements, and used Palm Island as a place for isolating "troublesome" individuals. The DNA did not allow white people to visit the settlements, except by special permission. A number of mission stations run by various church organisations had the approval of the DNA; their operations, either by consent or coercion, vigorously conformed with the Acts.

At the inaugural meeting of QCAATSI in January 1958 two clergymen, the Rev. W.A. (Bill) Brown, an Anglican minister from Chelmer, and the Rev. R.E. (Ron) Pashen, a Presbyterian minister, were elected to the provisional committee. At its first meeting, the Rev. Brown, the secretary, arrived late. He had been held up by a phonecall from John Herbert, the state member for Sherwood, who had advised him to resign. Herbert said he had been contacted by Special Branch police, who told him the organisation was being run by Communists and offered as proof the fact that Alec McDonald had done some preparatory secretarial work. By this time Alec had signified his unwillingness to serve in any active way on the Council because of other commitments. The Rev. Brown decided not to be frightened away from an involvement he regarded as his duty as a citizen and servant of his church, but very soon after this he was transferred to Casino, where he continued to work for the civil rights of Aborigines in northern New South Wales.

By the time Kath started attending meetings, the Council had a regular venue which had been offered by the Friends' Religious Society of Quakers. They owned a modest Meeting House on North Quay and both executive and general meetings of the Council were held there. One Friends' member was Fred Harris, who became a regular attender at meetings and a dedicated supporter.

Initially, the meetings were reasonably harmonious but, within a matter of weeks after the Rev. Brown's departure, the president, Dr

Stephen Fisher, also left Brisbane, and meetings started to become unpleasant. Underlying tensions between those who genuinely supported civil rights for Aborigines and those who wanted to preserve the status quo paralysed the Council's activities. It was not easy to tell who supported reform and who didn't, except for the Rev. Pashen and another clergyman, the Rev. Sweet (they really had those Trollopian names), both of whom unequivocally supported the status quo. One or other of them was forever warning the meeting not to "rock the boat", claiming how much better he knew and understood "these people". The Aborigines were not ready for the sort of responsibilities the Council was so foolishly trying to thrust upon them, they said. Theirs were the unctuous voices of extreme paternalism.[1]

A quieter, but equally regular, attender was an official from the DNA. Though he said little, he was perceived as a conduit to the department and to the minister, Dr Henry Winston Noble. Another attender, though an irregular one, was Joyce Wilding, well known to some QCAATSI members as a person who gave practical help to Aboriginal people in personal distress. She received government financial help to set up a hostel for destitute Aborigines.

The need to help her and the hostel was constantly raised at QCAATSI meetings by supporters of her objectives. No one in QCAATSI wished to discourage the brave and determined efforts of her and her associates in alleviating the distress of poor, dis-advantaged Aborigines who came to her hostel. No one wished her to withhold whatever comforts she could provide. Her charitable intentions, however, were evidently perceived by the government as a way to direct the energies of well-intentioned activists into politically meaningless channels. Those who had responded to Ada Bromham's call to set up a lobby for political reform had no wish to be deflected from that purpose, which had been central to the establishment of QCAATSI.

Muriel Langford, one of Joyce Wilding's keen supporters, also joined QCAATSI. It later became apparent that she was using her influence to cause trouble between the Queensland Council and FCAATSI. As she was also a member of the Women's Christian Temperance Union, like Ada

Bromham, there was considerable irony in this situation. (Where were you, Ada Bromham, when QCAATSI needed you!) In 1959 Alastair Campbell left Brisbane to take up a more senior position in the Repatriation Department in Melbourne. At that time I was a member of the executive of the Council, but in the following year I went to England for twelve months. Some very strange developments took place in Queensland in 1960 within the Aboriginal advancement movement.

By this time FCAATSI was a fast-growing organisation, most of its growth coming from South Australia, Victoria and New South Wales. State and federal politicians were becoming aware that it was a pressure group to be reckoned with. The FCAATSI executive, perceiving that the Queensland Council lacked political clout – a regrettable matter in a state with a large Aboriginal population and extremely repressive laws – decided to hold the Easter 1961 conference in Queensland.

It was with considerable dismay that organisers found that their letters to the Queensland Council were not being answered or even acknowledged; it was later believed that they had been passed directly to the DNA. Clearly, in 1960 plans were afoot to thwart the meeting of FCAATSI in Brisbane. With QCAATSI evidently not co-operating with the executive of FCAATSI, a new organisation was needed and it had to be set up quickly.

Gordon Bryant, a federal Labor MP keenly interested in Aboriginal advancement, came to Queensland and contacted some of the academics who had collaborated with Alastair Campbell on the Western Suburbs Branch booklet. Two of them, John Keats and Max Poulter, were members of the Toowong Branch of the ALP. This was a large, very active branch, and it was a relatively easy task to mobilise many interested members into assisting FCAATSI to hold the conference in Queensland.

Toowong Branch initiated the action and, very soon, the Queensland Aboriginal Advancement League (QAAL) was formed. Full co-operation with FCAATSI was assured and planning went ahead. Kath joined QAAL, so she had now committed herself to two organisations aiming to support Aboriginal advancement. The 1961 federal conference was to launch her into the struggle for the rights of Aboriginal people.

The conference was an unequivocal success. QAAL did an excellent job and the venue, one of the large lecture rooms at the University of Queensland reserved for the biggest classes, was crowded for almost all of the sessions. Delegates from southern states who had come hardly knowing what to expect were exceedingly pleased.

During the conference, the negative attitudes of some members of QCAATSI became obvious. They constantly spoke or voted against motions that would facilitate Aboriginal rights and decrease paternalistic control—and they were entirely unsuccessful.

With hindsight, it can be said that the most significant outcome of the conference was the alarm it had apparently caused in the DNA: it had tried to sabotage the conference and, thanks to QAAL, had failed. In May, at QCAATSI's first post-conference meeting, the Council unanimously reaffirmed its affiliation with the federal body; there was a feeling of exhilaration among committed members. It was at this time, too, that Dr H.W. Noble, Minister for the DNA, gave the signal that QCAATSI was arousing anxieties in the department. In a speech at a meeting of the Queensland Council of Social Service (QCOSS) he announced to the audience of social workers that there was now an organisation to help Aborigines which people of goodwill could readily support without fear of political stigma. This organisation was called the One People for Australia League (OPAL) and its founder was Joyce Wilding.

It was unfortunate that at this time Royce Perkins resigned as secretary. At the June meeting, Muriel Langford nominated a complete newcomer, Joe Cranitch, for the position of secretary, and this was seconded by the Rev. Pashen. A bemused membership allowed him to be elected unopposed. Another new member appeared on that night – George Cook, a public servant known to be active in the right-wing National Civic Council.

Matters came to a head at a meeting in July. Some thirty people poured into the little hall of the Friends' Meeting House – perhaps they had hired a bus. At Mr Cook's behest, each paid the ten shilling individual membership fee and so had immediate voting rights. The Council's open-to-all membership policy was backfiring badly. The DNA tactics were carefully timed, and their information was always accurate. The now overfilled hall proceeded with the meeting and when Joe Cranitch moved that the Council dissolve itself, the motion was carried.

Members of the old genuine Council stayed behind sadly in the hall. What was to be done? Fred Harris, a quiet, steadfast member of QCAATSI, said on behalf of the Friends that the hall would still be available on the usual evenings. We subsequently discovered that even the small sum of money we had collected to finance the newsletter and donate to Joyce Wilding's hostel had been handed over to the Justice Department on the very next day after this astonishing meeting.

It was necessary to revitalise QCAATSI and re-establish strong links with FCAATSI; its firm supporters continued to meet each month to discuss the ways and means. Kath sought advice from a solicitor, who told her the president should be asked to call a special meeting. The president, who had been elected in 1960 on the nomination of Muriel Langford, was an Aborigine, Sylvia Cairns. She had probably been made uncomfortable by the role thrust upon her before and after the FCAATSI conference.

The request for a special meeting was made but Sylvia did not respond. Kath's solicitor advised that this left the way open for us to institute other procedures which would enable us to make a new start with our old name. In early December a special meeting was called to reinstate QCAATSI as a full affiliate of the federal body; a few of the old schemers turned up, but they had no effect on the proceedings. Royce Perkins was elected president, Kath Walker was elected as secretary, and I as assistant secretary. So began my close working relationship with Kath, and our enduring friendship.

Some people belonging to the Council thought that Kath would be a token secretary and that I would do the real work, but this was far from the case. I couldn't even type! We worked together in harmony, communicating mostly by telephone. Clicks and other noises on the line suggested that our conversations were being bugged; and on one occasion a man even interrupted us to make some rude remarks.

Kath came to know and respect many other members of the reconstituted state Council, and was pleased by the variety of their backgrounds and political opinions. Royce was a staunch supporter of the Liberal Party and a devout Baptist; Eunice Gilmore, a librarian, had no political affiliations but a very deep concern for human rights, as had George Spall; Mrs Hoey was a Quaker from a well-to-do family; Mrs Young of the Women's Christian Temperance Union, disgusted by the behaviour of her fellow temperance worker, stuck with Kath and the Council. Fred Harris was a friend in every sense of the word; Elsie Gibson of the Union of Australian Women would go to any amount of trouble to further the ends of the Council; Dr Lilian Cameron, one of the authors of *The Aborigines and Torres Islanders of Queensland*, attended meetings with great regularity, as also did Daisy Marchisotti, a member of the Communist Party and great worker for the cause. The Queensland Trades and Labor Council kept its promise and always sent a representative; in 1961 and 1962 this was Wal Stubbings, whose contributions were always constructive (he was later replaced by Harry Gurnett, a consistent attender). Rodney Hall was already known to Kath through her involvement with the Realist Writers. It was a sufficiently diverse group to suggest that genuine interest in Aboriginal rights was felt in many different sections of the community.

Rodney Hall undertook the editing of the Council's newsletter, presenting it in such a way that it would be read and understood by Aboriginal people on reserves and missions and those living on urban fringes. He wrote with a simplicity and directness that clearly hit the mark, for the newsletter began to be smuggled on to the reserves. Readers' responses provided QCAATSI with shocking evidence of violations of the most basic human rights. A response of a different kind to the newsletters was the attempt to silence the editor by scare tactics. As well as being vilified in the more conservative journals, Rodney Hall was subjected to the visitation of a man who took up position across the road from his home with a gun across his knees.

Kath was also impressed by the regular attendance at the Council's monthly meetings of the federal member for the electorate of Brisbane, Manfred Cross. He was a sincere advocate of Aboriginal rights, and Kath thought he was very courageous to associate himself publicly and consistently with an organisation that had been so often smeared as pro-Communist.

QAAL continued to function after the Easter conference and Kath still attended its meetings. Members had observed with mounting horror the tactics employed by the DNA to dismantle QCAATSI. QAAL brought in an amendment to its constitution requiring all members to sign a declaration that they were not working for the DNA or any of the church-run missions. John Keats, another of the authors of *The Aborigines and Torres Islanders of Queensland*, was an active, enthusiastic member of QAAL.

It may be difficult in the 1990s to believe that the Department of Native Affairs in the 1960s could have been so strongly opposed to Aboriginal rights that they would resort to the tactics described above. The Queensland Act of 1939 was oppressive legislation. It infringed the Universal Declaration of Human Rights on all of the following counts.

- The Director, appointed by the Minister for Native Affairs, oversaw the administration of policy throughout the state and had authority over administrators on settlements, mission superintendents and local protectors (usually policemen). The Act stated: "The Director shall establish on any settlement or mission reserve an Aboriginal Court constituted by the Director or in his absence the protector or superintendent or other person appointed by the Director" and: "There shall be established at every settlement and mission reserve a gaol or lock-up."

- The Director was the legal guardian of all Aborigines under the age of twenty-one.

- The Director was empowered to move Aborigines from any reserve to any other reserve and to empower any person acting under his authority or any officer of police to arrest individuals and move them to other reserves.
- Aborigines could not leave reserves, settlements or missions without permission.
- The Director or his representative were empowered to remove children from their parents. The Director could arrange adoptions to anyone he considered suitable.
- The Director could withhold permission for one Aborigine to marry another Aborigine or a non-Aborigine.
- Personal property could be seized and the right to protest was denied; mail was subject to censorship.
- All or part of wages or other monies were paid into a bank account in Brisbane; Aborigines were not issued with bankbooks and had to obtain the local Protector's permission to draw out any amount up to twenty pounds (more required the Director's permission).[2]

Perhaps it was the awesome inhumanity of the Act that made the DNA so sensitive to criticism.

While Kath was taking on great responsibilities in the fight for civil rights for her people, she maintained her interest in writing poetry. She continued to attend meetings of the Realist Writers, where she met interesting people such as John Manifold, already an established writer. She was having difficulty finding the right voice in her poetry and one well-meaning member of the group took one of her poems, rewrote it in his own style, and sent it to the *Bulletin*. It was published as Kath Walker's poem, and Kath felt angry and humiliated.

One evening she rang me and asked if I would go with her to see James Devaney. He had heard her recite a poem at a meeting and had

Kath promotes her
second volume of poetry,
The Dawn Is At Hand,
Bathurst, 1966.

offered to talk to her about developing her ability. Kath didn't know much about him, except that he was a poet, and she wanted me to come along to his inner-city flat as a sort of chaperone. He was a charming elderly man and he and his wife were most gracious. He gave her the advice and help she knew she needed and had been seeking for years. As the Realist Writers had done, he told her she must read lots of other poets; but, unlike them, he explained to her why. Learn what to look for in other people's poetry, he suggested; know the poetic conventions of the time, and see how they are used in the expression of ideas. He made it clear to her that modern poetry allowed her more freedom than she seemed to believe.

Kath went away to experiment with free verse, rhyme scheme, and line length, no longer constrained by outmoded ideas. *We Are Going* (1964), her first collection, sold more than ten thousand copies in seven editions. James Devaney wrote in the Foreword:

> Kath Walker is the poet of her people. Song makers there have always been among them, long before the colonization of this country. Now for the first time the Aboriginal poet is articulate in English...Kath Walker is to be welcomed into our national literature.

The Dawn Is At Hand (1966) sold almost seven thousand copies in two editions, and in 1967 won the Jessie Litchfield Award for literary merit. *My People* (1970) sold more than eight thousand copies in three editions. Kath's literary reputation quickly spread beyond Australia, her poems were translated into a number of languages and invitations to visit and lecture around the world flowed in.

Her poetry owes everything to her Aboriginal heritage. As discussed in the next chapter, among Kath's forebears were a Scotsman, a German, and a Spaniard and she was as accurately acquainted with her ancestry as the most blue-blooded of English duchesses once were. Of it all, however, it was her Aboriginality that she was proudest to claim – or perhaps the Aboriginality insisted on claiming her. A strong sense of Aboriginal identity inspired all that she wrote and, in turn, led her to declare for equality for all peoples: as she says in a poem "I'm for humanity, all one race".

LEFT: Founding publisher of Jacaranda Press, Brian Clouston, first met Kath when *Overland* editor Stephen Murray-Smith brought her to his party. When Kath sent him her poetry manuscript he passed it on for appraisal to publisher's reader Judith Wright. The rest is history: *We Are Going* (1964) was Australia's first published volume of poetry by an Aboriginal writer.

ABOVE: With Kath at Lennon's Hotel, Brisbane to celebrate the launch of *We Are Going* are, from left, Eunice Hanger, Frank Thompson and Judith Wright.

LEFT: While visiting Australia in 1966 Soviet poet Yevgeny Yevtushenko invited Kath to the USSR, but it was to be twenty years before she went there, and at the invitation of President Gorbachev.

BELOW: At the 1966 Adelaide Festival, poet Ian Mudie provides a desk for Kath as she signs a volume of her poetry for writer Eugene Lumbers.

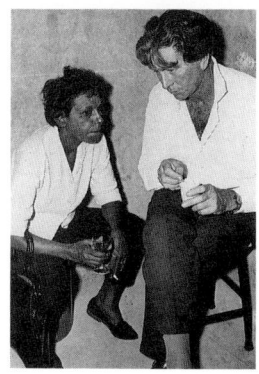

LEFT: Time out at the Adelaide Festival in 1966. Kath talks to poet Roland Robinson, who was deeply interested in Aboriginal lore.

MEETINGS • 39

In his 1965 report to the FCAATSI annual meeting, Joe McGinness of Cairns, a most determined advocate of his people's rights, acknowledged the importance of Kath's poems in inspiring Aboriginal advancement movements. This was only one aspect of their importance. Her great friend, the poet Judith Wright McKinney, has written a literary appreciation of Kath's poetry, which appears in Part Two of this book.

With *We Are Going*, Kath was often accused of not being its author. For one who had worked so hard at her writing the attempts to deny her voice authenticity were hurtful. In the seventies, after she had returned to live at Stradbroke, she put this denigration of her creativity into a broader context:

One thing that happens when you have a bit of white blood in you and have a bit of white education is that when you misbehave people say, "Aha, that's the Aboriginal in you" and when you accomplish something they will say, "Aha, that's the white coming out in you." It happened as a child and it still happens.[3]

Praise and encouragement came from white people Kath knew she could respect. In 1962 she visited Dame Mary Gilmore, then aged ninety-four. She had some of Kath's poems in front of her – sent, it seems, by James Devaney – and she asked Kath to read them to her. She told her they were beautiful and that Queensland poets had a duty to see them published. Kath modestly disclaimed, "I don't think they're good enough," to which Mary Gilmore replied, "These poems belong to mankind. You are the tool that writes them down."

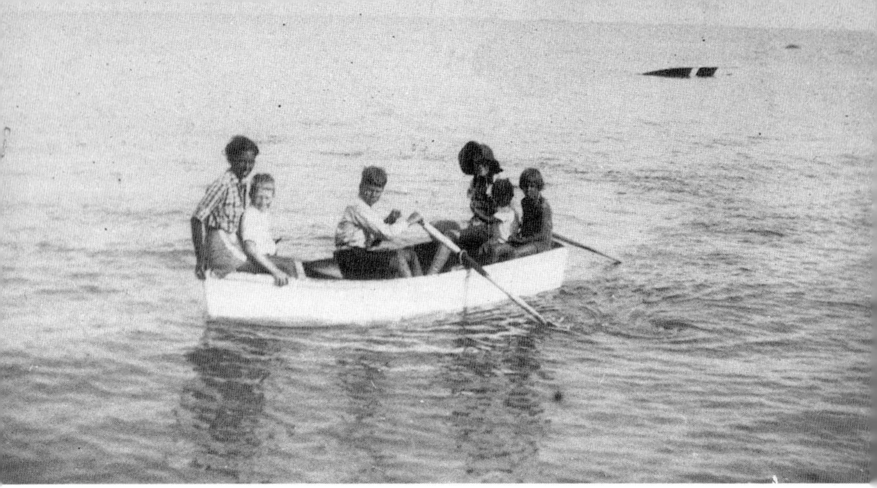

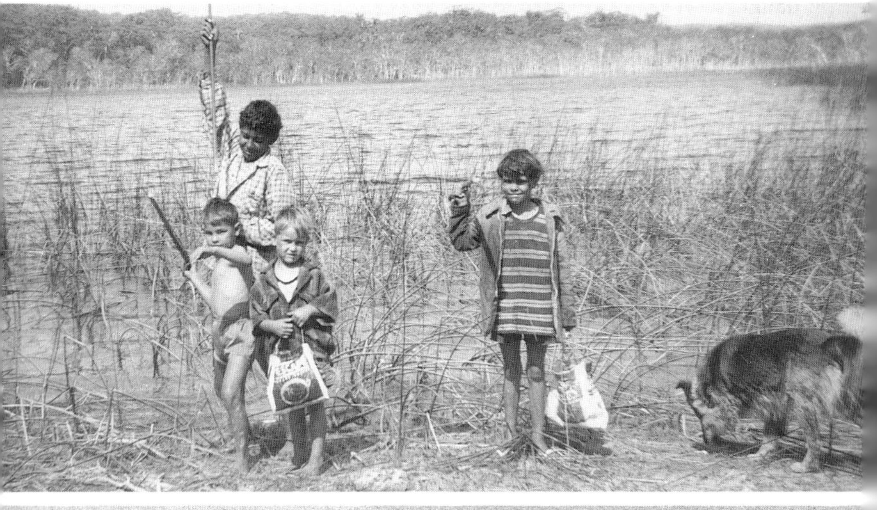

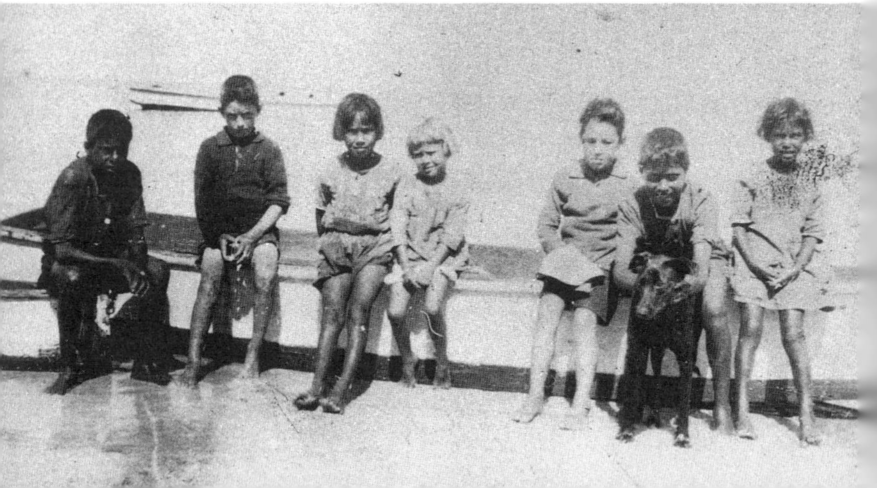

Relations

They had been there for as long as anyone could remember, the Noonuccal people of Minjerribah. They had not been driven away by the white invaders and there were still many descendants on the island now known as Stradbroke. Among the inevitable marriages or matings with whites, a certain man named Gonzales took a Noonuccal mate, and their daughter was Kath's grandmother. She herself married a Captain Frederic Ruska, a German, and had four children with him: Edward (Kath's father), Ernie, Rebecca and Emma. She died while they were still quite young, and Frederic married a white woman. When she discovered that Frederic's first wife had been an island Aborigine, she wrapped herself up in a blanket soaked in kerosene, lit a match, and burnt to death.

For Captain Frederic Ruska the solution to his problem of having no one to look after his children was not difficult. Aware that the Noonuccal people would care for them, he took them to Amity Point, left them there, and returned to the mainland. The four children were loved and taught and became steeped in the ways of the Noonuccal people. Edward, or Ted as he was known, never thought of himself as anything other than a Noonuccal Aborigine.

There are now many people who identify themselves with pride as Aborigines. Having been gladly accepted and cared for by Aborigines, they indeed belong to that large and welcoming family.

Young Ted Ruska and his brother and sisters felt wholly committed to their mother's Noonuccal family group, from whom they learned to fish and hunt. Young Kath told many stories about the ways she learned these skills from her father.

Simple, enduring
pleasures of life on
Stradbroke.

Kath's father Ted Ruska lived and worked on the island for most of his life. *"He'd...walk home and tell me that Mrs So-and-so said you walk this land as though you think it's yours. 'It is mine, isn't it?' And he'd say, 'Yes girl, and don't you forget it.'"*

Kill to Eat

My father worked for the Government, as a ganger of an Aboriginal workforce which helped to build roads, load and unload the supply ships, and carry out all the menial tasks around the island. For this work he received a small wage and rations to feed his seven children. (I was the third-eldest daughter.) We hated the white man's rations – besides, they were so meagre that even a bandicoot would have had difficulty in existing on them. They used to include meat, rice, sago, tapioca, and on special occasions, such as the Queen's Birthday festival, one plum pudding.

Of course, we never depended upon the rations to keep ourselves alive. Dad taught us how to catch our food Aboriginal-style, using discarded materials from the white man's rubbish dumps. We each had our own slingshots to bring down the blueys and greenies – the parrots and lorikeets that haunted the flowering gums. And he showed us how to make bandicoot traps: a wooden box, a bit of wire, a lever on top and a piece of burnt toast were all that was needed. Bandicoots cannot resist burnt toast. We would set our traps at dusk, and always next day there was a trapped bandicoot to take proudly home for Mother to roast. Dad also showed us how to flatten a square piece of tin and sharpen it. This was very valuable for slicing through the shallow waters; many a mullet met its doom from the accurate aim of one of my brothers wielding the sharpened tin. Dad made long iron crab hooks, too, and we each had a hand fishing-line of our own.[1]

Ted went to school at Myora, the old mission site several kilometres north of Dunwich, until Grade Six. At age ten he worked on the mainland on a sheep run, and then became an oysterman travelling the coast. After his marriage, he worked for the Queensland government at roadmaking, and as a cargo handler for the steamship *Otter*. Although exempted from the Queensland Acts, he was classified as an Aboriginal

Colour Bar

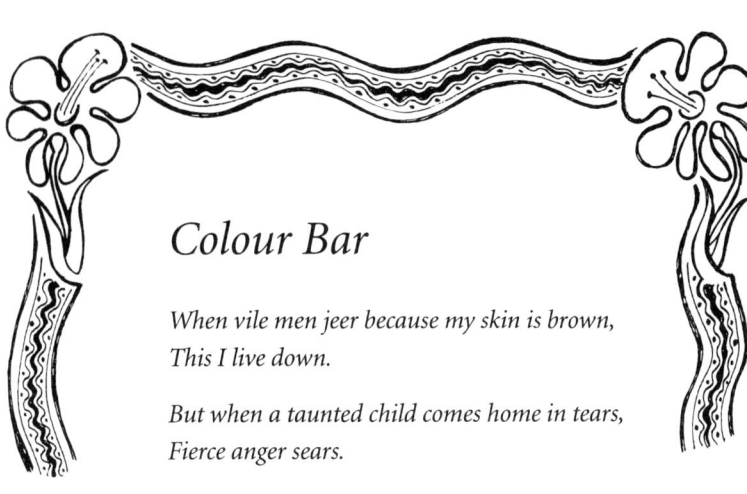

When vile men jeer because my skin is brown,
This I live down.

But when a taunted child comes home in tears,
Fierce anger sears.

The colour bar! It shows the meaner mind
Of moron kind.

Men are but medieval yet, as long
As lives this wrong.

Could he but see, the colour-baiting clod
Is blaming God

Who made us all, and all His children He
Loves equally.

As long as brothers banned from brotherhood
You still exclude,

The Christianity you hold so high
is but a lie,

Justice a cant of hypocrites, content
With precedent.

employee and paid only one pound a week, plus rations. He fought for, and obtained, two pounds a week for Aborigines not under the Acts.

There was a strong colour bar on the island, but during the war this was largely broken down by black and white women working together on welfare committees. During this time Ted clashed frequently with his manager, a white man who knew next to nothing about roadmaking or cargo-handling. When this man ordered the men to work through their lunch-break, Ted objected, was rebuked and then resigned. Consequently the men refused to work for the white foreman. The manager reported this to the Health and Home Affairs Department in Brisbane and was told: "Reinstate Ted Ruska and respect his wishes from now on."[2]

Kath's mother Lucy experienced a very different and much less benign upbringing. She too was born of a white father and an Aboriginal mother. Her mother, Minnie, worked on a large station at Marion Downs in central Queensland and her father, named Alexander McCullough, had emigrated from Scotland. Lucy was still a little girl when Alexander died. Not much later some people arrived in a dray and asked her if she would like to go for a ride. Her mother was not at home just then, and knew nothing of this visit. It was a very long ride for the ten-year-old girl that day. She never saw her mother again.

She was brought to Brisbane and placed in a Catholic "home" for uncontrollable girls. Here she was taught to wash and scrub, cook, iron, and recite prayers, but not to read or write. At fourteen, she was assigned to domestic service in Brisbane, and a few months later was sent to work as a housemaid on a large station near Boulia. On one occasion the station's mistress took her to faraway Maryborough to help on a shopping expedition, and there she met Ted Ruska.

Ted later wrote to her, proposing marriage, and was puzzled when he received no reply. He wrote again, and Lucy summoned enough courage to ask one of the station hands to read the letter to her. She used the same good offices to "write" her acceptance. Lucy and Ted married and went to live on Ted's beloved Stradbroke Island – a strange and novel environment for a girl who had spent her short life on cattle properties and in a Catholic institution.

When she worked at the station, her wages were banked by the Department of Native Affairs and she was given a small sum of pocket money. After her marriage Ted asked for her money to be paid to her, only to be told that Lucy had spent it all. No bankbooks had been issued and no other records were accessible.

Never having been taught to read and write was an omission in her "education" Lucy could never forgive. Kath's sister Lucy told me that her mother's resentment at her illiteracy was always an issue when the family was growing up and that Lucy was extremely anxious for all of them to read and write. When Kath's first book, *We Are Going*, was published in 1964, it was one of the happiest days in Lucy Ruska's life.

This is my land. I have always said that, even as a child. The white people used to say to Dad: "That girl walks this land as though she thinks it's hers." Dad wouldn't say anything – he'd just walk home and tell me that Mrs So-and-so said you walk this land as though you think it's yours. "It is mine, isn't it?" And he'd say, "Yes girl, and don't you forget it".[3]

Kath was very conscious of her Noonuccal ancestry and felt a particular involvement with Myora because of its early reputation as a "sitting-down place", a place for quiet contemplation, and its later use as a mission. In earlier days some Aborigines had been removed from Myora and housed on crown land not far away at One Mile, just north of Dunwich. In the early 1960s there was a threat to evict them and Kath decided to take a group of sympathetic white people across to the island to assess the situation. She was particularly keen that Manfred Cross

The Teachers
For Mother, who was never taught to read or write

Holy men, you came to preach:
"Poor black heathen, we will teach
Sense of sin and fear of hell,
Fear of God and boss as well;
We will teach you work for play,
We will teach you to obey
Laws of God and laws of Mammon…"
And we answered, "No more gammon,
If you have to teach the light,
Teach us first to read and write."

Lucy Ruska, at home.
All her life she resented
never having been taught to
read and write.

should be one of them, probably hoping that he could exercise some political clout to establish the right of the people to remain where they were. Bob and I were also invited, as was Alastair Campbell, who happened to be visiting Brisbane.

On our visit to the island we were excited to meet Kath's relations and friends and we were shown around the places that belonged to her real home. Kath also took us to visit her mother; Ted had died in 1954. Lucy Ruska was a small robust-looking woman who seemed quite relaxed at having her kitchen invaded by so many strangers. She told us, with some amusement, the story of how she came to have a plentiful supply of heavy grey blankets. When Queensland became a separate colony in 1859 and chose its royal name, Queen Victoria decreed that each year on her birthday all Aboriginal women in the state should receive a blanket. (Unfortunately Aborigines in Victoria received no such favour when that state was named – though the royal beneficence might have been of more use to them.)

Another visitor especially invited by Lucy Ruska was Granny Sunflower, a well-known personality on the island and its last wholly Noonuccal survivor. She was a lively person who spoke freely and happily; in her young days she travelled quite widely on the mainland with a group who sang and told stories to Aboriginal audiences. She told us one of her stories, a legend about two boys who disobeyed their elders by going into forbidden territory and so were turned into a double-pointed headland. Granny Sunflower had the story-teller's gift of holding her audience rapt. The story was clearly new to Lucy who, when it ended, shook her head sadly and said, "Poor little fellows." Granny Sunflower, "last of the Noonuccals", died in August 1964.[3]

Alastair Campbell, Granny Sunflower, Kath's sister Florrie Ruska, and her mother Lucy Ruska at One Mile in about 1962

Gooboora, the Silent Pool
For Grannie Sunflower, Last of the Noonuccals

Gooboora, Gooboora, the Water of Fear
That awed the Noonuccals once numerous here,
The Bunyip is gone from your bone-strewn bed,
And the clans departed to drift with the dead.

Once in the far time before the whites came
How light were their hearts in the dance and the game!
Gooboora, Gooboora, to think that today
A whole happy tribe are all vanished away!

What mystery lurks by the Water of Fear,
And what is the secret still lingering here?
For birds hasten by as in days of old,
No wild thing will drink of your waters cold.

Gooboora, Gooboora, still here you remain,
But where are my people I look for in vain?
They are gone from the hill, they are gone from the shore,
And the place of the Silent Pool knows them no more.

But I think they still gather when daylight is done
And stand round the pool at the setting of sun,
A shadowy band that is now without care,
Fearing no longer the Thing in its lair.

Old Death has passed by you but took the dark throng;
Now lost is the Noonuccal language and song.
Gooboora, Gooboora, it makes the heart sore
That you should be here but my people no more!

Dugong Coming!

Old Sammy of Myora was the catcher of dugong…

As soon as we saw the shirt waving in the breeze, we would scatter in all directions calling out to the women, "Dugong coming!"

The women would stop whatever they were doing, grab their dilly-bags and sugar-bags, and take off for the cutting-up and sharing-out place at Myora.

By the time all the tribe had assembled, the dugong would be lying on the sand at the foot of Gapembah Hill. The kids would be teasing each other and yelling their heads off, while the women gossiped in the shade of the big mango-tree. The men would be grouped around the dugong, and Sammy would be instructing them where to place it ready for the cutting-up…

My mother had seven children and was always happy when Sammy threw into her bag part of the grumpii – the intestines. She would take home the precious meat, trusting us to help her with the heavy load, but she always carried the grumpii herself. I think she felt we might lose it.

As soon as we arrived home, she would light up the wood stove and then prepare the meat for cooking. Dugong meat looks very like beef, and Mother would roast it in the oven. She would wash the grumpii thoroughly in salt sea-water, then place it in a pot of water to boil on the stove until it was tender. After that it was allowed to cool while Mother minced up some of the flesh, and the heart and liver. This was all pushed into the grumpii, and the ends tied tightly with string, and it was then put into a pot of water once more and boiled. We called it grumpii sausage. In later years I had the opportunity to taste Scots haggis, and found it not unlike our dugong sausage. I enjoyed the taste of haggis as much as I liked our grumpii.

Today, when the white man's food is eaten so widely by Aborigines, the tribe no longer hunts the dugong. They believe that to hunt dugong when their bellies are full would be to act against the natural law of "kill to eat". They believe that the Good Spirit would punish them severely if they killed dugong out of greed – and that the Good Spirit might take one of the tribespeople to even the score.

This paperbark tree on the shores of Brown Lake, Stradbroke Island, was a favourite childhood spot for Kath. When she returned to live at Moongalba in the 1970s she visited it often.

The dugong still feed in Moreton Bay, and I am sure they must wonder what has become of their enemy, the black man. Sometimes, in July, when I see the chewed weed floating ashore on the high tide, my mouth waters for the taste of dugong. But the law of the tribe is good, and no one intends to break it just because of a longing for what used to be.[4]

In 1963 Lucy became ill and had an operation for bowel cancer, which left her with a colostomy. When she was discharged from hospital she went to Kath at Myrtle Street. In those days there was little post-operative help available and Lucy was terribly distressed by her inability to manage the stoma. Kath discovered, by trial and error, dressings and bindings that would protect her mother's clothing and contain the odour. Lucy learned to manage these for herself and returned to Dunwich. She died on 19 September 1966 and, like Ted, was buried in the Dunwich cemetery.

Kath had always been puzzled by her mother's attitude to Roman Catholic doctrine. Lucy had not been treated well by the nuns and she knew that the "education" she had received from them had equipped her only for domestic drudgery. She did not try to bring her own children up as Catholics though she was anxious for them to accept Christian teachings and to know the Bible. Towards the end of her life, she turned back to the church that had somehow given her faith.

In 1974 Kath wrote a short sketch in the *Sunday Sun* of 10 November describing a woman's religious experiences that moved from early acceptance through doubts, some anger and many uncertainties to a final return to her Catholic faith. It was a sensitive and moving account and it ended with the line: "I know all this because that woman was my mother."

The house was left to Eddie, who returned to live on the island after the war, as did Eric. Ted and Lucy had seven children, but one of them, Hector, had died at nineteen, when Kath was nine. Florence (Florrie), the eldest child, lived on the island all her life. When she married (and became Florence Coolwell), Ted "gave" her a block of land on which to build a house. (Of course Ted had no legal right to give away land as the Aborigines had never obtained title to the land at One Mile.) In 1976, when Eddie died, Florence moved into the old Ruska home, claiming possession, so to speak, by occupation.

Eddie had had two sons and a daughter, Elizabeth. After his death his sister Lucy took in Elizabeth and brought her up. Lucy married Arthur Pettit, a white man who enlisted in the Second/Twenty-fifth AIF Battalion in the Second World War. He died in May 1983 and since then the battalion has kept in touch with Lucy and been concerned for her welfare. After her marriage Lucy lived in Brisbane, but she has always been a frequent visitor to the island and has kept up her enthusiasm for fishing. Lucy has two daughters of her own, Judy and Erica, as well as her "adopted" niece Elizabeth.

In 1994 the only surviving children of Ted and Lucy were Lucy Pettit and, youngest of all the children, Vivian, who married a white man and seldom returned to visit her birthplace.

By 1961, Kath was deeply committed to Aboriginal advancement. Her sons were aged fifteen and eight, and she was a single, Aboriginal mother living in a predominantly white suburb. With the new demands that were

Author Kathie Cochrane, centre, with her children Tom, Jane and Bill and Kath Walker with Vivian and Denis in 1961

being made on her, the stresses must have been enormous. It was a large sacrifice for her to leave her children in the care of friends and relatives while she journeyed round Australia in second-class railway carriages and slept in spare beds in the homes of well-wishers. I remember her telling me that Denis said to her: "You might be a good mother but you're a pretty rotten father"; she felt that Denis resented her separation from Bruce. In more mature years, he told her that at school he had been more ostracised for being a fatherless child than for being Aboriginal.

When Denis turned sixteen in 1962, Kath got him into the merchant navy, with considerable help from the Seamen's Union. She hoped that this would provide him with a secure future and independence from the mother he resented. She also hoped that his emancipation into a working life would help him develop the leadership qualities she recognised in him. Unhappily for her, and for Denis himself, he became increasingly aligned with movements such as the Black Panthers which advocated violence as a solution to racial inequality. He adopted aggressive postures, and became involved in confrontations that ended in brawls. Eventually he was arrested and gaoled for violent behaviour, and Kath grieved deeply.

With Vivian, the sixties were altogether different. Of dissimilar temperament to Denis and seven years his junior, he was of an age to get on with my children, Jane, aged eight, and Tom and Bill, aged eleven – and get on with them he did! When Kath attended conferences or went on tour, Bob and I often took him into our family; Denis was at sea by this time. Vivian's equable nature made him a favourite with everyone who looked after him. His Aunt Lucy loved him dearly. Elsie Gibson, of QCAATSI, enjoyed his company. Winnie Buzacott, an old friend, found him a delightful companion at her Tweed Heads acreage by the lake; and we enjoyed his company in our home at Sherwood.

Son of Mine
(To Denis)

My son, your troubled eyes search mine,
Puzzled and hurt by colour line.
Your black skin soft as velvet shine;
What can I tell you, son of mine?

I could tell you of heartbreak, hatred blind,
I could tell of crimes that shame mankind,
Of brutal wrong and deeds malign,
Of rape and murder, son of mine;

But I'll tell instead of brave and fine
When lives of black and white entwine,
And men in brotherhood combine –
This would I tell you, son of mine.

Vivian, aged about ten

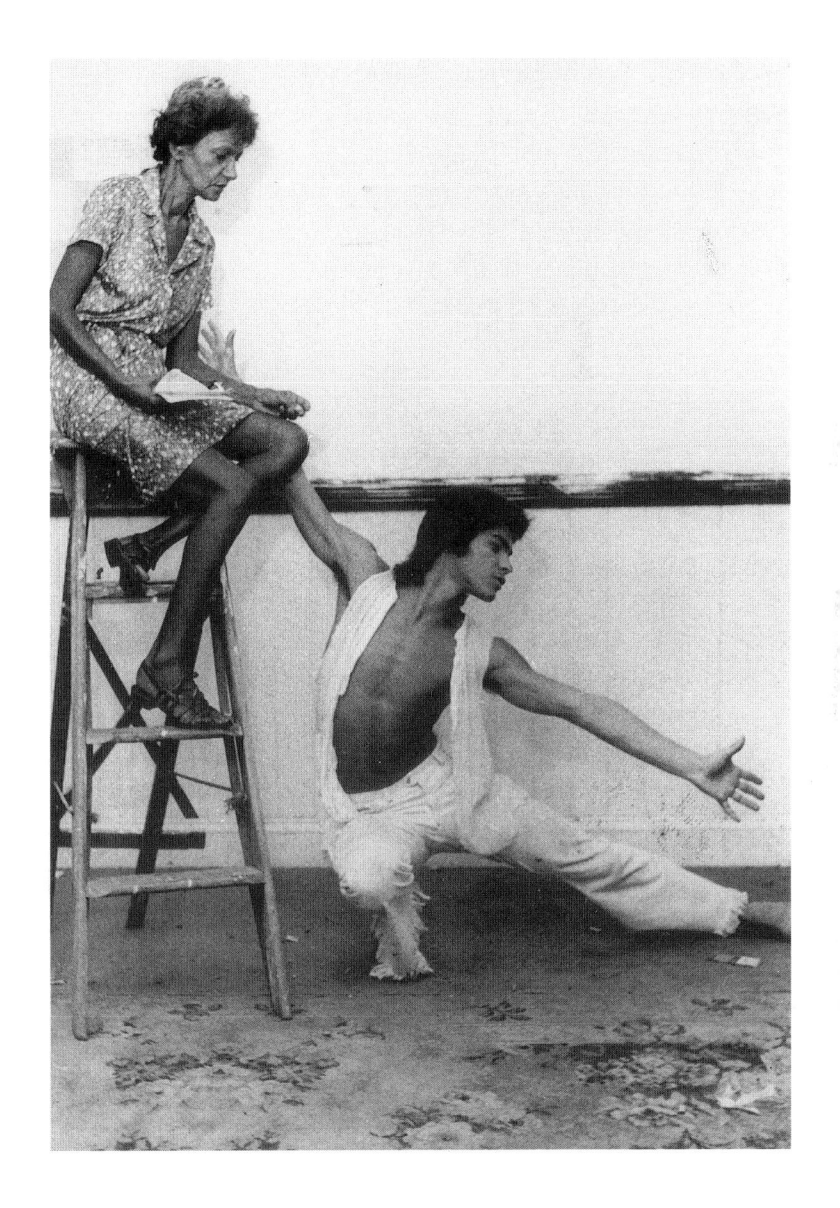

Kath helps Vivian
rehearse for a
performance
in Sydney.

Integration – Yes!

Gratefully we learn from you,
The advanced race,
You with long centuries of lore behind you.
We who are Australians long before
You who came yesterday,
Eagerly we must learn to change,
Learn new needs we never wanted,
New compulsions never needed,
The price of survival.
Much that we loved is gone and had to go,
But not the deep indigenous things.
The past is still so much a part of us,
Still about us, still within us.
We are happiest
Among our own people. We would like to see
Our own customs kept, our old
Dances and songs, crafts and corroborees.
Why change our sacred myths for your sacred myths?
No, not assimilation but integration,
Not submergence but our uplifting,
So black and white may go forward together
In harmony and brotherhood.

While staying with us once, Vivian accidentally broke Jane's collarbone and insisted on accompanying us on visits to the orthopedist to share in the long waiting-room vigils; this was typical of Vivian.

As he grew older, Vivian's interests in drama and dancing became apparent, and he showed great promise in both. On his own initiative, he gained a place at the National Institute of Dramatic Art (NIDA) in Sydney in 1969. Kath was delighted, but after only three months he rang to say he could not stay the course. He felt stifled by rigid procedures that seemed to him to be casting all the students into one mould. This was a disappointment to Kath, but a harder blow was to come when he told her that he was homosexual; she was stunned.

As she battled on through the sixties, her dedication to the civil rights movement was interwoven with her ambition to gain a better world for her sons, and also for her grandchildren, the first of whom was born in 1965. Denis married a white girl, Patty, and they had three sons, Raymond, Joshua and Che and a daughter Petrina. Kath was anxious for them to grow up with an awareness of their Aboriginal inheritance and a tolerance of other people's beliefs. Her concern for children was not sentimental; she believed they had potential as agents for change, provided they received the appropriate messages from the adult world: "So black and white may go forward together/In harmony and brotherhood."

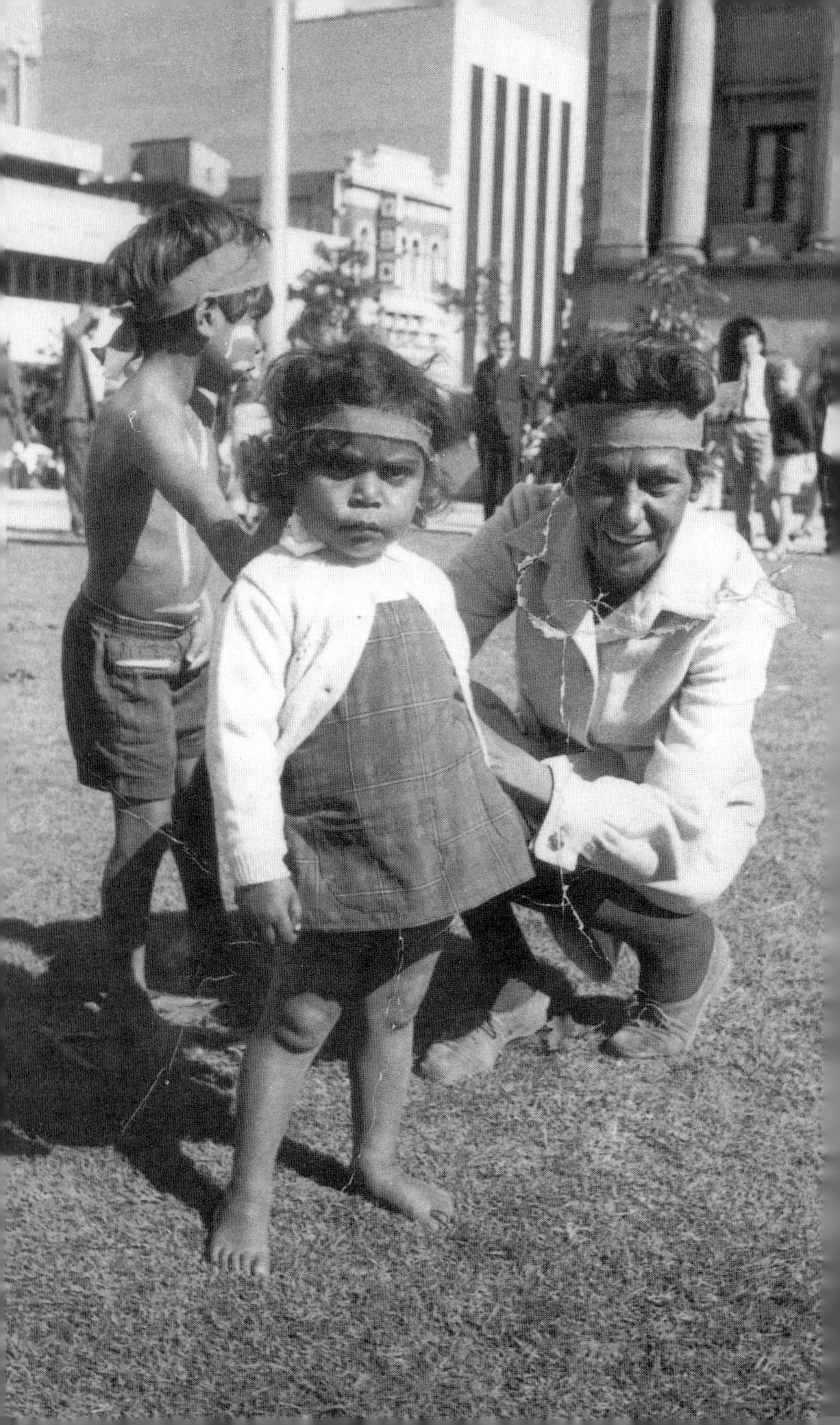

Protest!

Although in the 1960s the Vietnam War was the focus of protest movements in Australia and the United States, people had also begun taking to the streets about the destructive practices of miners, loggers and building developers. World-wide protests about the slaughter of whales resulted in the closure of the great whaling station at Tangalooma, on Moreton Island, in 1962. Racial discrimination was increasingly denounced and the denial of basic human rights for Australia's Aboriginal people became a prominent issue.

At the 1962 Easter conference of FCAATSI, Kath was elected as Queensland secretary. She read the poem "Aboriginal Charter of Rights", which she had written for the occasion: "Must we native Old Australians/ In our own land rank as aliens?" The timing was of significance, for there was a groundswell of protest around Australia about the Aborigines' lack of citizenship.

At the FCAATSI conference in Brisbane the previous year, Kath had first met Faith Bandler, a delegate from Sydney. Faith's father was a Pacific islander who had been "black-birded" to work on the Queensland canefields early in the century.[1] The two women were the most outstanding speakers with black skin in the country, and had a shrewd grasp of what needed to be said on behalf of indigenous Australians.

Aboriginal lore denies women a dominant role in decision-making, which is why Kath always insisted on referring to herself as a spokeswoman and never consented to being called a leader. She was always reluctant to offend traditional taboos and thus cause dissension among her people.

"Where are we going to get our leaders from?" Faith asked Kath at the conference, the very question that troubled Kath herself for many years. The following year FCAATSI selected them to head a delegation to meet the prime minister, Robert Menzies.

Aboriginal Charter of Rights

We want hope, not racialism,
Brotherhood, not ostracism,
Black advance, not white ascendance:
Make us equals, not dependants.
We need help, not exploitation,
We want freedom, not frustration;
Not control, but self-reliance,
Independence, not compliance,
Not rebuff, but education,
Self-respect, not resignation.
Free us from a mean subjection,
From a bureaucrat Protection.
Let's forget the old-time slavers:
Give us fellowship, not favours;
Encouragement, not prohibitions,
Homes, not settlements and missions.
We need love, not overlordship,
Grip of hand, not whip-hand wardship;
Opportunity that places
White and black on equal basis.
You dishearten, not defend us,
Circumscribe, who should befriend us.

PREVIOUS PAGE:
At King George Square, Brisbane, in about 1970

"I feel as if they all
want a part of me,"
she often said.

Give us welcome, not aversion,
Give us choice, not cold coercion,
Status, not discrimination,
Human rights, not segregation.
You the law, like Roman Pontius,
Make us proud, not colour-conscious;
Give the deal you still deny us,
Give goodwill, not bigot bias;
Give ambition, not prevention,
Confidence, not condescension;
Give incentive, not restriction,
Give us Christ, not crucifixion.
Though baptised and blessed and Bibled
We are still tabooed and libelled.
You devout Salvation-sellers,
Make us neighbours, not fringe-dwellers;
Make us mates, not poor relations,
Citizens, not serfs on stations.
Must we native Old Australians
In our land rank as aliens?
Banish bans and conquer caste,
Then we'll win our own at last.

With her, at right, is
Pastor Doug Nicholls.

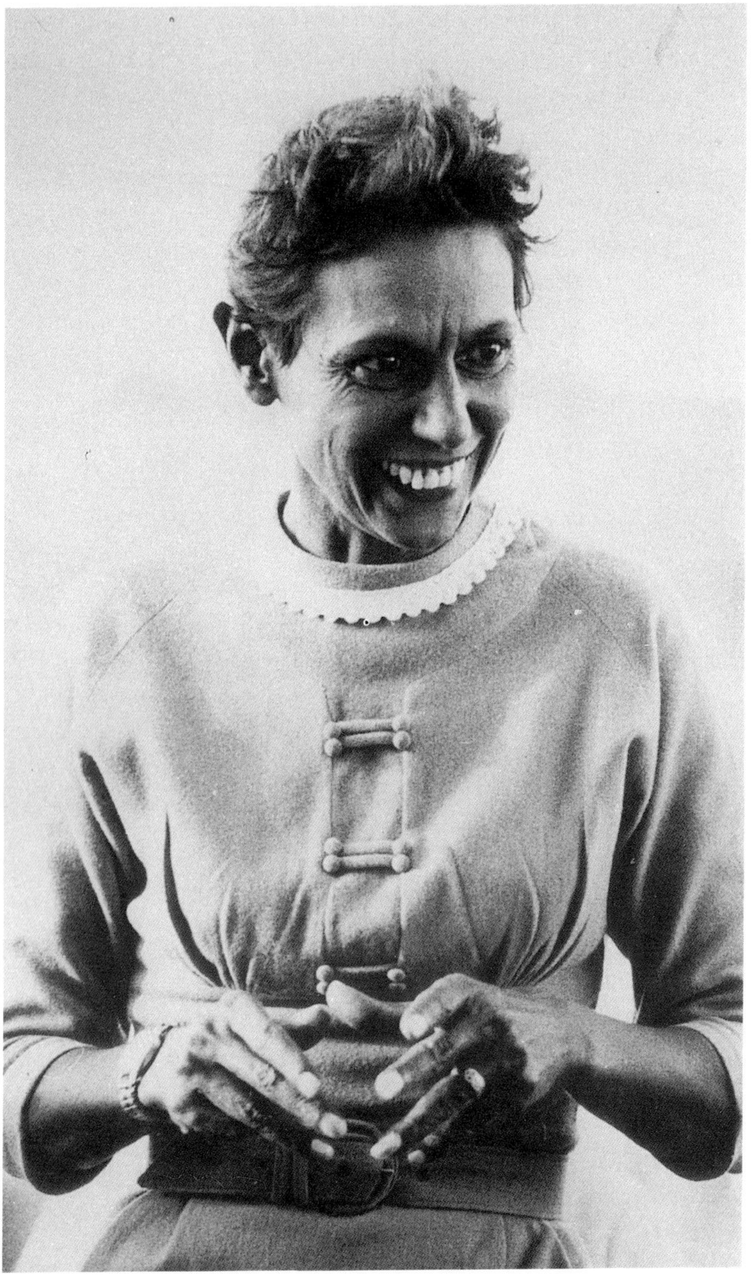

The delegation included four other Aboriginal people: Ted Penney (Western Australia), Dexter Daniels (Northern Territory), Pastor Doug Nicholls (South Australia), and Joe McGinness (north Queensland). The purpose of the meeting was to urge the prime minister to call a referendum among white Australians on whether or not Aboriginal people should be counted as citizens. It was worth a try, even though Menzies had declared he would never instigate another referendum after the government's resounding defeat on the anti-Communist issue in 1951.

Faith and Kath opened their case by detailing some of the worst consequences for Aboriginal people of current iniquitous state laws. At one stage during the interview, after Kath made some point, Menzies looked at her and said, "You must be the lady poet." She had referred to alcoholic drink as "white man's poison" and, when Menzies closed the meeting, he ushered his guests into a reception area where white-jacketed waiters offered refreshments. "I think it's time for a bit of white man's poison," Menzies said pointedly. The four men in the delegation asked for fruit juice; but Faith and Kath, appreciating that Menzies might feel uncomfortable drinking alcohol if all delegates refused it, asked for sherry. As Kath received her glass she remarked: "Do you know, Mr Menzies, that where I come from you could be gaoled for supplying alcohol to an Aborigine?" The waiters began to laugh but Menzies scowled at them. "I'm the boss here," he said and he poured himself a very large whisky.

Section 51 of the Constitution of the Commonwealth of Australia stated:

> The Parliament shall, subject to this constitution, have power to make laws for the peace, order and good government of the Commonwealth with respect to [then followed 39 clauses of which Clause 26 read]:
>
> The people of any race, other than the aboriginal race in any State, for whom it is deemed necessary to make special laws.

Section 127 of the Constitution provided that:

> In reckoning the numbers of people of the Commonwealth, or of a State or other part of the Commonwealth, aboriginal natives shall not be counted.

In 1962 a petition to the Commonwealth Government was launched that sought the removal from the Constitution of Section 51, Clause 26, and Section 127. For the purpose of rallying support for the petition the Victorian Aboriginal Advancement League arranged for Kath to make a six-week tour of all states. Extracts from the itinerary illustrate the hectic schedule:

Ballarat, Thursday, 16 October
1.40 p.m. Train departs Spencer St [Melbourne] for Ballarat
3.40 p.m. Arrive Ballarat
7.30 p.m. Public meeting
10.30 p.m. "Overlander" to Adelaide

Sydney, 9 November
10.30 a.m. Radio interview
11.30 a.m. Lunch-hour meeting
2 p.m. Interview, ABC radio
6.45 p.m. Channel Two

Scarcely had she set foot back home in Brisbane when a tour of north Queensland was organised for December. The Victorian Advancement League had not budgeted for this part of the tour and hoped that Queensland's two councils for Aboriginal advancement would be able to raise the necessary money. This was not possible, as QCAATSI had been left with hardly any funds, as has been noted, and QAAL was too new an organisation to have money to spare. Ingrid Palmer, an academic from the University of Queensland, came to the rescue with her holiday savings. Her generous gift was accepted by Kath with heartfelt gratitude. Enthusiastically she prepared for more travelling, more lecturing and more interviews.

Kath's tour was important to the advancement movement. She learnt much about conditions in the north Queensland settlements and had productive talks with Aboriginal activists such as Joe McGinness and Gladys O'Shane, who were anxious for the success of the referendum and enthusiastic about the efforts of FCAATSI. However, she was annoyed when her request for permission to visit the Yarrabah Aboriginal Reserve near Cairns was refused by the Department of Native Affairs. On 6 December the *Townsville Bulletin* reported:

> The secretary of OPAL (Mrs M. Langford) said today: "I think the Department was wise to refuse Mrs Walker permission. The Federal Council for Aboriginal Advancement looks for trouble rather than trying to help the Aborigines. Their business is trouble and why should it be stirred up at Yarrabah?"

Both the state and federal Councils were constantly accused of trouble-making—rocking the boat. Implicit in the criticism was the strong suggestion that the experienced people in charge of the Aboriginal settlements knew how to cope with the residents and keep things running smoothly. An example of this "smooth running" had come to the ears of QCAATSI from the Hopevale Mission in mid 1961.

Hopevale was a mission reserve near Cooktown run by the Lutherans. In this remote settlement, almost two hundred kilometres north of Cairns, Jimmy Jacko "went bush" with his girlfriend Gertie Simon. When another young man ran after them to tell Jimmy Jacko that his sisters were being punished on his account, the couple decided to return and apologise. Jimmy Jacko's apologies were brushed aside: he would have to work for two weeks without pay, after which he would be sent to Palm Island. In those days Palm Island, off Townsville, was a punishment place for Aborigines who did not submit to the discipline of other missions and reserves; it was also a threatened punishment for Aborigines not detained in reserves.[2]

Jimmy Jacko's immediate and humiliating penalty was to be publicly flogged with lawyer cane by fellow Aborigines. When they refused to do this, he was publicly flogged by the pastor/Protector of the mission. As for Gertie, her hair was shorn off in public view of all the residents. This outrageous overreaction to a minor misdemeanour was legal under the Queensland Acts.

No one will ever know how many acts of barbarism were committed on the reserves. This instance only came to public notice because of QCAATSI and its newsletter. An account of the incident was smuggled out to the Council, who passed it on to the *Courier-Mail* where it was

With Joe McGinness at a FCAATSI conference in the early sixties. Joe soon became a prominent speaker and in 1991 published his autobiography, *Son of Alyandabu: My Fight for Aboriginal Rights*.

published on 21 June. It was also reported to the Federal Council when Kath and Joe McGinness attended a meeting in Melbourne, and thereafter the case became known nationally.

Many other reports of ill-treatment of people living on reserves came to QCAATSI's notice. Some stemmed from the fact that Aborigines there were not permitted to control their own money. Without bankbooks they had little chance of knowing how much money they had. One case concerned a young mother at Woorabinda, a government Aboriginal reserve, who had a toddler and a baby but was refused permission to spend her own money on a pram. There were numerous reports of police

In the hectic sixties Kath made time for children whenever she could. Here she visits a school in Kempsey, New South Wales. *"It's the children who are innocent and ready to learn. It's the children who are the hope of mankind."*

brutality – particularly alarming considering that in many settlements the Protector was the local policeman. A report from Cherbourg concerned the brutal treatment of two teenage boys by Native Police on the night of 21 January 1966. It came with a number of signed statements and a petition signed by sixty-eight Cherbourg people. The Council organised a deputation of three – Kath Walker, Manfred Cross and Royce Perkins – to protest to the then Minister for Aboriginal Affairs, Jack Pizzey. They were given the usual assurances.

In addition to Kath's secretarial work for QCAATSI and FCAATSI, and her efforts to ensure that a referendum on Aboriginal citizenship would be held, requests for her to speak to all kinds of groups were being received. After the publication of *We Are Going* adult education bodies also invited her to give lectures to their mainly white classes not only about her poetry, but also about Aboriginal beliefs, customs and aspirations. She understood the importance of what she was doing and persevered in spite of adverse criticism from both white and black Australians. Many Aborigines accused her of walking away from her own people to work with the white "do-gooders". And some of her white supporters resented her extraordinary abilities and the growth of her popularity. These people referred to her sneeringly as a "black messiah". Such criticisms distressed Kath, but not for one minute did they deter her.

In 1964, when I was teaching at the Yeronga State High School, I asked the principal if I could invite Kath Walker to come and talk to one of my classes. He readily gave permission, and when the word got around other teachers said they would bring their classes. On the afternoon of Kath's visit three other teachers and I crammed our students into the room, where they sat on desks, floor, windowsills – wherever they could. This didn't worry Kath at all. She had every bit as much skill as Granny Sunflower in holding her audience spellbound. For her, educating and entertaining were one and the same thing; she was very effective. Her reputation as an excellent communicator with school children spread quickly and many requests came to her to visit schools all over Queensland and in New South Wales. The remuneration was always meagre and the payment often slow, but she never refused a request if she could possibly fit it in. For her the education of the young was a bridge to racial understanding.

Education departments must revise their out-of-date, mid-Victorian criteria. When tutors from other countries and Aboriginal elders from this country, through cultural exchange, are recognised and their true worth recognised in universities and schools, then we will have, and will be able to boast of, a truly multicultural society.

Australian educational institutions can and must lead the way in forcing parliaments to recognise these urgent needs. Concurrently, our universities must acknowledge and recognise the fact that their domineering and entrenched elitism still implements the mid-Victorian attitude of "survival of the white tribe at any cost" and is counter-productive to a racial equality of the future.[3]

It became increasingly difficult for the Queensland government to ignore Kath. The DNA had denied her access to Yarrabah in 1962, but in 1964 she was asked to be part of a team with two other women to visit and report on six settlements in north Queensland. This DNA initiative was largely due to the persistence of Fred Bromley MLA, an enthusiastic supporter of Aborigines. With her were Peg Whiley, a social worker employed by the government, and Mrs Lawrie from Westwood, whose husband was a federal senator. Yarrabah was one of the settlements they visited. Their report to the DNA was not made public, but by the end of 1964 it was known that new legislation to replace the 1939 Act was being drafted. Kath reported to QCAATSI on the grossly sub-standard conditions she had witnessed on the settlements on all fronts: housing, health, and education.

The new act, *The Aboriginal and Torres Strait Islanders' Affairs Act*, appeared early in 1965. Kath was then acting editor of the QCAATSI newsletter, and in the March/April issue she commented:

Changes are so meagre that most of the oppressive features of the old Protection Acts remain. It makes no proposals regarding wages and conditions, housing, voting rights, training, education, titles to lands and community development.

QAAL was also strongly critical of the new act. Spokesman John Keats pointed out that a number of its provisions fell short of the United Nations Declaration of Human Rights and he moved a motion to condemn the act at the 1965 FCAATSI conference.

The repressive powers of the act and its use in thwarting the aspirations of people living on reserves were well illustrated twelve years later in 1977 when the Aborigines living at Aurukun and Mornington Island made a strong bid for greater self-management. They were publicly and enthusiastically supported by the Uniting Church, which

Assimilation – No!

Pour your pitcher of wine into the wide river
And where is your wine? There is only the river.
Must the genius of an old race die
That the race might live?
We who would be one with you, one people,
We must surrender now much that we love,
The old freedoms for new musts,
Your world for ours,
But a core is left that we must keep always.
Change and compel, slash us into shape,
But not our roots deep in the soil of old.
We are different hearts and minds
In a different body. Do not ask of us
To be deserters, to disown our mother,
To change the unchangeable.
The gum cannot be trained into an oak.
Something is gone, something surrendered, still
We will go forward and learn.
Not swamped and lost, watered away, but keeping
Our own identity, our pride of race.
Pour your pitcher of wine into the wide river
And where is your wine? There is only the river.

was in charge of these missions; and the Rev. Sweet, now in authority at the reserves, was particularly outspoken on their behalf. The Queensland Acts were invoked against them and Russell Hinze, the Minister for Local Government, appointed "council officers" who would ensure that attempts at real self-management were thwarted. The people then appealed in a submission to the federal government. The Commonwealth Department of Aboriginal Affairs issued an information paper, entitled "Aurukun and Mornington Island", which stated:

> The [Queensland] Acts and accompanying regulations as they stand bestow extensive powers on the State Director of Aboriginal and Islander Advancement and other officials, in particular the Managers of Queensland Aboriginal reserves.
>
> Nothing like the Queensland Acts exists in any other state or territory.

Menzies kept his promise of never having another referendum, but in 1967 Harold Holt succeeded him as prime minister and scheduled the referendum for May of that year. Kath became campaign director for the Yes case for Queensland which, of course, involved her in more speech-making and the preparation of Vote Yes propaganda. More than 90 per cent of white Australians recorded a Yes. Aboriginal Australians were now officially citizens of the Commonwealth. It was, at least, a beginning.

In April 1968 Kath moved house to 46 Raff Avenue, Holland Park, having known for some time that her home and others in Myrtle Street were to be bulldozed to make way for the Southeast Freeway. Soon after moving in to her new address a woman came up to her and told her that "a lot of other women" were wondering if she drank methylated spirits. Kath smiled politely and replied, "No, as a matter of fact I don't. But if I'd known that all you people did I'd have thrown a party."

Her new local electorate was Greenslopes, a seat that had been held for the Liberal Party by Keith Hooper since 1957. With the next state election

Kath leaves her Holland
Park home for the World
Council of Churches
meeting in London
in 1968.

due soon, Kath accepted endorsement as the local ALP candidate. Neither she nor the party had high hopes of success in that blue-ribbon electorate, but Kath believed that Aborigines should be making their presence felt in political circles.

The people of Australia gave the Government the go-ahead at last year's referendum but so far we have heard lots of words and have seen very little action... As a young person I found myself objecting not only to the subservience that native Australians were subjected to at the hands of the whites, but also to the way that my own people accepted this as their fate.[4]

The time had come for Aborigines to enter the political arena and, as Kath put it, "show our black faces in Parliament". She was concerned, too, that many politicians supported the idea of assimilation for the Aboriginal people: they should adopt the white man's way of life and so become, as it were, black white men; why should they want to preserve an Aboriginal identity? Standing for Parliament gave Kath a chance to put her views on this denial of the right of Aborigines to be Aboriginal and be proud of it. The state election was held in May 1969 and Kath was not elected, but she had made her point.

That same month she went to London. The World Council of Churches had invited her to be a delegate at their Consultation on Racism to take place there. Of all the delegates, she was the only Aboriginal Australian and the only female Australian. (Don Dunstan, later premier of South Australia, also attended: he had been actively involved with FCAATSI from the beginning.) Kath was now aged forty-eight, and was unrivalled in her experience: she had been a victim of racism herself; knew of her mother's deprivations; knew from her travels around Australia the different shades of discrimination that existed among the states; and had brought the plight of the dispossessed Aborigines to the notice of the world through her poetry.

A Song of Hope

Look up, my people,
The dawn is breaking,
The world is waking
To a new bright day,
When none defame us,
No restriction tame us,
Nor colour shame us,
Nor sneer dismay.

Now brood no more
On the years behind you,
The hope assigned you
Shall the past replace,
When a juster justice
Grown wise and stronger
Points the bone no longer
At a darker race.

So long we waited
Bound and frustrated,
Till hate be hated
And caste deposed;
Now light shall guide us,
No goal denied us,
And all doors open
That long were closed.

See plain the promise,
Dark freedom-lover!
Night's nearly over,
And though long the climb,
New rights will greet us,
New mateship meet us,
And joy complete us
In our new Dream Time.

To our fathers' fathers
The pain, the sorrow;
To our children's children
The glad tomorrow.

If she was just coming to prominence internationally at this time, her Australian reputation was already soaring, as evidenced by the multitude of requests and invitations she was now receiving. She often told me how hard she found it to say no. Fame may be a spur, but it can also be a fearsome burden. "I feel as if they all want part of me," she used to say.

In February 1970 she wrote to federal MP Mr W.C. Wentworth, accepting an invitation to join the advisory board of the newly established Aboriginal Aged Persons Home Trust. It is clear from the correspondence that the position involved more than sitting in a boardroom or making phonecalls; in April 1970, for example, Kath went to Cunnamulla to discuss appropriate housing requirements with civic authorities and local Aboriginal communities.

In September she was elected as president of the Aboriginal Publications Foundation, an organisation that encouraged creative writing and the arts among Aborigines. It commissioned and published original work, provided scholarships, conducted competitions and exhibitions, and organised training classes. A typical extract from her appointments diary shows her commitments for a four-month period in 1971. Clearly the demands on her time and energy had become absurd.

13 April – 8 May	Adult Education lecture tour, Western Australia
10 May	Aboriginal Council for the Arts, Sydney
21 – 23 May	New Guinea book promotion
25 May	Visits to Wollongong and University of NSW
28 May	Aboriginal Publications Foundation meeting, Sydney
31 May – 12 June	Adult Education tour, Victoria
12 – 17 July	Adult Education tour, Tasmania

PROTEST! • 79

By the late sixties, Aboriginal people were aware that they had substantial support among white Australians in their demands for civil rights. The enormous Yes vote of the 1967 referendum must have been a most heartening experience for Aborigines, dispossessed of their land since 1788. Ten years had passed since Ada Bromham's efforts had succeeded in establishing a Queensland movement for Aboriginal civil rights, and now the indigenous people were anxious to form their own organisations.

In 1969 Kath told me with some pride that a Brisbane Aboriginal and Islanders Tribal Council had been formed. This was just what she had worked so hard for and for which she had endured the accusation of "walking away" from her own people. Surely this was what we had all been working for. Was it not time for a white-dominated organisation to bow out?

At one of our monthly meetings at the Friends' Meeting House in 1969, I gave notice that I would move at the next meeting that we disband our organisation in order to channel our energies into supporting the new Tribal Council. The foreshadowed motion encountered overwhelming opposition from the white members present. One incident was particularly devastating. Alec McDonald had kept his promise to try to see that some trade union person would always be a member of the Council. There had been several representatives over the years, most recently Harry Gurnett from the Postal Workers' Union.

Harry Gurnett was a keen, well-intentioned supporter of the Council and its aims, attending its fundraising functions as well as the monthly meetings. Yet, though his support for QCAATSI seemed genuine, when I formally read out my motion, he objected that the Council couldn't hand over matters to Aboriginal people. "We've made Kath Walker what she is" he said. Everyone was startled. Kath's response was immediate. She rose from her secretarial chair, thanked Mr Gurnett very much, and walked out. And that was that.

From then on Aborigines abandoned QCAATSI and joined the Tribal Council. Many who had refrained from joining QCAATSI became active in the new organisation, which informed the general secretary of

FCAATSI that it would not affiliate with the federal body unless the voting rights were vested in the Aboriginal and Islander people and in them only. The Victorian Aboriginal Advancement League was much inclined to go along with this idea.

By 1970 the number of Aborigines in all states involved in the struggle for Aboriginal rights had risen greatly. They now constituted a significant proportion of conference delegates. At the July 1969 executive meeting of FCAATSI, Kath presented a case for an Aborigine-controlled organisation. The proposal was circulated and brought forward for discussion at the thirteenth annual FCAATSI conference held at Easter 1970. Her arguments were strong and clear:

If black Australians are to become masters of their own destiny white Australians must recognise them as being capable of formulating their own policy of advancement. Prior to the white invasion of this country, history tells us black Australians had a high standard of moral and social pattern behaviours. White Australians must understand that "what is good" for them does not necessarily follow as being "good" for black Australians. Coalitions cannot work effectively nor can they be sustained on the moral, friendly or sentimental conscience of white behaviour patterns.

White "goodwill" is a shaky foundation on which to build. White Australians, if they wish, can withdraw the "goodwill" and black Australians can then be back where they started and have gained nothing for themselves. Black Australians must strengthen themselves into a solid, determined fighting unit and dictate their own terms for their own advancement. They must define what is best for their own advancement and then they can determine where white Australians can be of assistance. Unless they take this line, black Australians will always be cast in a beggar's role, with a second-class status.

There is no reason why white lawyers cannot defend black Australians in courts. There is no reason why white Australians cannot support black organisations. This then is the supportive role white Australians can play. Only when black and white Australians can accept each other as co-equal partners who identify their goals as politically and economically similar can there be a healthy coalition. Black and white Australians can work side by side provided they set up, recognise and respect each other's sets of values. Then, and only then, can black and white work together in full balance and respectful harmony for a bigger and better Australia for all Australians.[5]

As the conference progressed it became apparent that Kath's powerful statements were a catalyst in the growing divisiveness within FCAATSI. The Easter 1970 conference was, in the words of one member, Barrie Pittock, "traumatic, exhausting and highly emotional". Many rumours and accusations of plots to eliminate FCAATSI were circulated among bewildered delegates. In a paper written in the aftermath of this most disturbing of FCAATSI conferences, Pittock summed up the opposing viewpoints: on the one hand was the liberal humanitarian group, supported mainly by trade unionists, and on the other a large minority group of Aborigines and Torres Strait Islanders. Each side sought to make its own voice dominant.[6]

Once again, as in Queensland, trade unionists were determined not to let Aborigines take charge of their own civil rights movement. The minutes of the FCAATSI executive of 18 March 1970 record that John Baker, the FCAATSI trade union co-ordinator, reported: "The Victorian government is subsidising bus-loads of Aborigines from Melbourne to FCAATSI conference…Victorian and Commonwealth governments are arranging this in order to eliminate Federal Council."

Thus was misrepresented a modest subsidy from the Victorian government to help a busload of Aborigines to attend the 1970 Easter conference. There was also a reference to my well-intentioned motion to disband QCAATSI, which was made to appear as some sinister plot against the Aboriginal rights movement. Some Aborigines did not know whether to vote for Aboriginal control of FCAATSI or to vote to preserve the status quo. The more experienced and politically aware among them, however, felt that the time had come for them to assume full control over their civil rights movement. What the issue boiled down to was: would white people continue to dominate and control the movement, or would they now hand over that control and that domination to the Aboriginal people themselves?

Kath with boxing
champion Lionel Rose
and John Moriarty in
the late sixties

Paternalistic attitudes can only perpetuate paternalistic relationships because white Australians persist in fooling themselves that they are "doing for black Australians". They refuse to believe that black Australians can "do" for themselves.[7]

From this time on, FCAATSI, QCAATSI and other councils that had been initiated by enthusiastic and sympathetic white people declined and disappeared. This was a most important development in the movement for Aboriginal rights, and the part that Kath had played had been of enormous importance. The decade had begun with her as one of the very few Aborigines capable and willing to speak out for the rights of her people. Her potent voice and energetic involvement had been an inspiration to fellow Aborigines and to white sympathisers. People, black and white, who had been involved in the advancement movements of the sixties had no cause to regret their well-meant efforts. They had taken a first, highly effective, step in laying a foundation for Aborigines to articulate their own demands for civil rights.

Early in 1971 a young white man, a representative of ABSCHOL (a scholarship scheme for assisting secondary and tertiary Aboriginal students) came to Kath and told her that she was considered too old to be of further use to the Tribal Council. His name was Alan Dubov – a name she never forgot. If she had perceived him as a brash, inexperienced young white man, she would not have been concerned, but she knew he was a messenger from the young Aboriginal men of the Queensland Tribal Council. The hurt bit into her deeply.

At this time her health was poor: she was suffering from chest infections for which she would not seek medical advice. Vivian got in touch with the family doctor: "Mum is walking round with pleurisy," he said. Kath knew she was exhausted and depressed, and it was not hard for Vivian to convince her that she would be wise to sell her Holland Park house and go back to live on Stradbroke Island.

"Aboriginal poet, Kath Walker, has withdrawn from public life to her birthplace," announced the *Australian* on 8 June 1971. Kath resigned from all the committees she had worked so hard for, and withdrew from an Adult Education Literary Fund tour arranged for May and June. But in July she went to Hobart to fulfil some public-speaking engagements. It was not in her nature to retire from the struggle for Aboriginal rights and Aboriginal dignity.

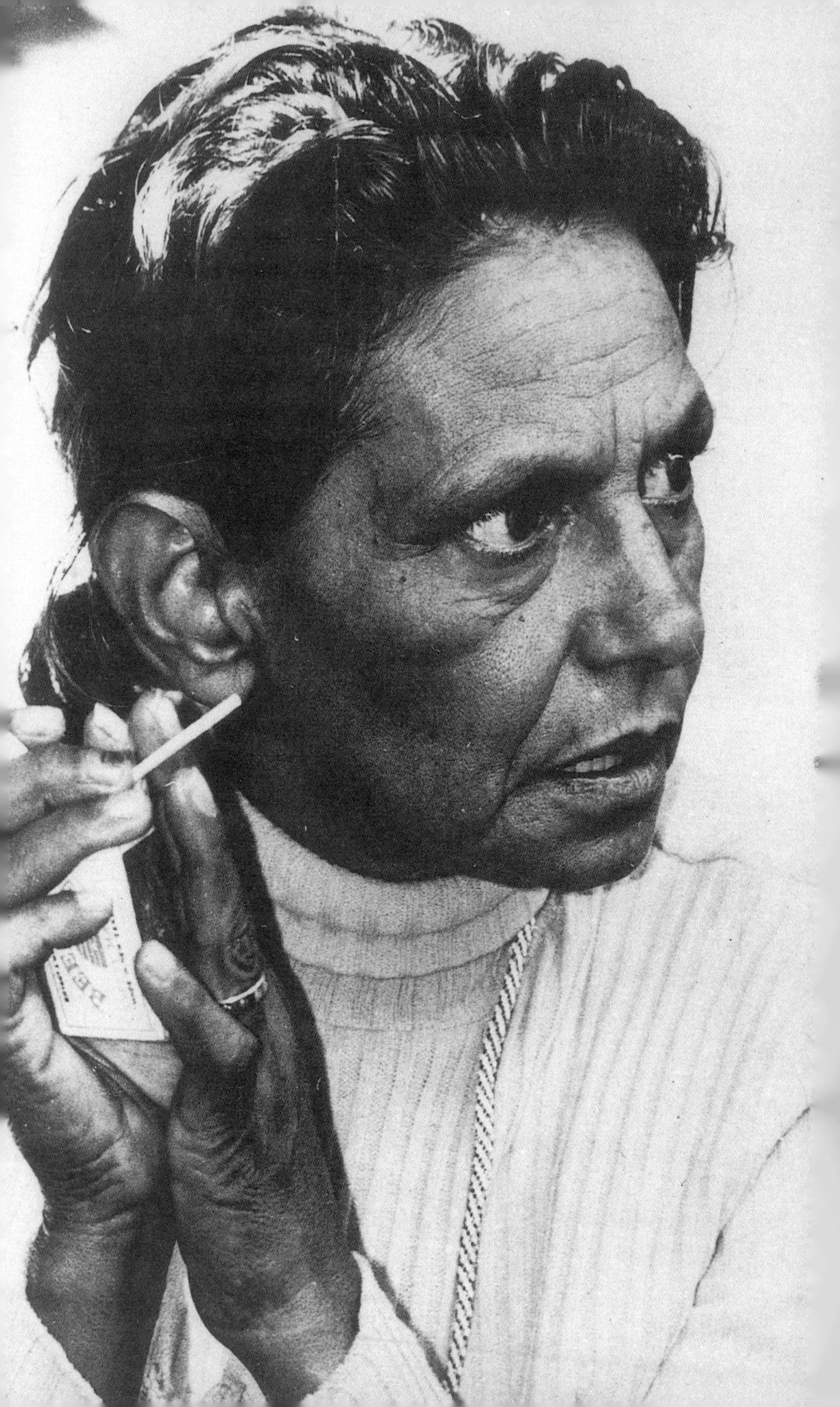

Moongalba

Mirrabooka

Biami the good spirit was kept very busy, guarding the tribes as they roamed throughout the earth, and he was very much troubled for them. He found that he could not watch over all of them at once; he knew he must have help to keep them from harm.

Among the tribes there was a man called Mirrabooka, who was much loved for his wisdom, and the way in which he looked after the welfare of his people. Biami was well pleased with Mirrabooka, and when he grew old, Biami gave him a spirit form and placed him in the sky among the stars, and promised him eternal life. Biami gave Mirrabooka lights for his hands and feet and stretched him across the sky, so that he could watch for ever over the tribes he loved. And the tribes could look up to him from the earth and see the stars which were Mirrabooka's eyes gazing down on them.

When in later times white invaders came from across the sea and stole the tribal lands, they did not know that this group of stars across the southern sky was Mirrabooka, and they renamed them. They called Mirrabooka by the name of the Southern Cross. And the eyes of Mirrabooka they called the Pointers. But it is really Mirrabooka there, stretched across the sky; he will be there for ever, for Biami has made it so.[1]

Kath went home to Minjerribah, across the waters of Quandamooka (Moreton Bay), and selected an area where she wanted to live and develop an educational centre. The place she chose was of considerable significance to her, as it was to all the descendants of the Noonuccal tribe. Kath liked to tell the following story.

"There was once an elder of the tribe who was usually to be found near the tip of the island now known as Amity Point. When he was confronted with a difficult problem on which he had to adjudicate, he would walk south to a quiet piece of land near a swamp, and there he would sit down to think the matter through in solitude. His name was Moongalba, and this place became known as Moongalba's sitting-down place.

"Now when the Roman Catholic missionaries came to the island in 1838, they saw no hope of bringing Christian salvation to the people if they were to continue wandering about the island, fishing, hunting and gathering food for themselves. The missionaries told them they must choose one area that would become their permanent place for living. The people chose Moongalba's sitting-down place, and it was here (just north of Dunwich), that the mission established a church, a school and a cemetery.

"The priests told the people that they were living in sin and insisted that they wear European clothes and go through a marriage ceremony with their partners and say prayers every day. So every day the Noonuccal people gathered at the mission church, and one of the prayers they said was the Lord's Prayer. Some of the older women began to ask questions about "daily bread" and wondered where it would come from. From Heaven, they were told. But no bread came, however hard they prayed. Eventually, some of the elders called a big "talk-talk" at a midden site about a mile south of the mission, and they decided the missionaries were not telling them true things. The old men told the women to discard their clothes and throw away their wedding rings and soon the people drifted back into their old familiar habits and dispersed over the island."

Kath's father was one of a group of young men who later decided to settle at the One Mile, as it became known, and it was here that he subsequently built the family house. Kath would tell how Ted and Lucy kept digging up the gold-plated lead wedding rings that the women had discarded.

Myora...

Myora, years ago, was an Aboriginal mission station on Stradbroke Island, and some Aborigines were placed under what was known then as the "protective custody" of the missionaries. These missionaries were sent from the mainland; usually they were volunteers who believed that the Aborigine was in need of their Christian guidance. Each time a new missionary arrived at Myora, he would be of a different denomination from his predecessor, and once a student of Buddhism arrived. We children would follow him into the bush, where he would hide little carved idols in the branches of the trees. The white man called the place Myora, probably because he had misinterpreted the Aboriginal name, which is Moongalba.[2]

In 1842 the missionaries next attempted to establish a mission at One Mile, but this also failed. These failures help to explain why the Noonuccal people of Stradbroke Island escaped the harsh impositions of the Queensland Acts and were thus able to live in their natural family groups. Some missionaries continued to work on the island for many years, but they were independent of the dictates of the Acts. The continuing cohesion of the Noonuccal people places them in a strong position to lay claim to ancestral land, as they can prove, as required, their continuous occupation. In this they are more fortunate than the descendants of their former neighbours on Moreton Island, who were all driven off their ancestral land in the last century.

In 1971 Kath made a verbal application to the Queensland Lands Department for the lease and eventual purchase over twenty years of five acres (two hectares) at Moongalba for the purpose of establishing a museum and art gallery. The suggestion was made to her that the land be leased only and that she should present a written submission to the Redland Shire Council. The submission, dated 21 October 1971, refers to the lot of land as Myora, the name given to it by the mission. It states: "it is my intention to convert this land, should the Redland Shire see fit to grant my request, into a historical museum, library, art gallery and park." This expressed her long-cherished hope for a permanent establishment on the minimally alienated land, as enduring evidence of Aboriginal customs and values. Judith Wright understood Kath's motives well:

> Working, talking, writing, travelling, learning about the culture that had once existed and seeing what its loss had done to her people, she saw the need for a revival of pride in their race and tradition, and for education in that culture for the whites who had dispossessed them. She began to plan for some kind of centre, some focus where Aborigines and Torres Strait Islanders could come together in a place of their own and begin to assert their own value. Somewhere to learn, as she had, about the depth of their roots in the past, and to see themselves as they really were, not as rejected social outcasts but as people suffering a deep wrong, and with a culture to identify them.[3]

Kath's known association with the island, as well as her reputation as a poet and Aboriginal activist, almost certainly worked in her favour when she asked the Redland Shire Council to allow her to use the land at

Relaxing with Denis at Moongalba

Thousands visited Moongalba each year, black and white, among them students, campers and holiday-makers.

Moongalba. Nevertheless, permission was given reluctantly.

The application for permanent ownership was rejected, but the Redland Council granted her a twenty-five year lease at peppercorn rent; this was later extended to her lifetime. The provisos showed an outrageous lack of comprehension of the scope and nature of the proposals. For example, one condition was: "All persons coming onto the property to be clean and not intoxicated; fires to be lit only with proper permission" – in other words, through their European eyes, they envisaged a sanitised "blacks' camp".

Kath had not been idle while waiting for permission to use her selected area of land. Although unable to proceed with professionally designed and constructed permanent buildings, she erected, at the spot where the sandy path from the land met the bitumen road, a sign saying: Moongalba, Sitting-Down Place; and she built a gunyah for herself from tree branches and pieces of canvas. The land sloped gently and many willing volunteers helped her to clear about half the site of scrub and replant it with some two hundred trees and shrubs. The habitat of resident birds, lizards and small marsupials was respected. A band of trees at least a hundred metres deep was left undisturbed along the road on the side boundary to shut out the busy world and preserve the tranquillity within.

ABOVE: Sketching
LEFT: At Brown Lake, Stradbroke Island, Kath Walker and author Kathie Cochrane

Vivian, Kath and
Denis at Moongalba

While hoping for permission for more permanent buildings, Kath organised the building of some open-sided sheds. The site was ideally suited to incorporate an outdoor theatre, for which Kath made curtains of threaded seashells. Saturday classes for children of the island offered painting, drawing and theatre activities. At craft sessions children learnt how to use ready-to-hand natural materials, absorbing the while the wisdom of conservation.

Soon primary and secondary schools from the mainland were seeking permission to bring their students across the bay to experience all there was to see and do at Moongalba. Large numbers of children came. Before long Kath was organising holiday camps for underprivileged children, some of whom came from rural areas in northern New South Wales, others from the poorer suburbs of Sydney. She welcomed the opportunity to teach them how to be self-sufficient: they cooked their meals under her guidance, pitching their tents and finding out about Aboriginal ways of obtaining food. Between 1972 and 1977 more than eight thousand children visited Moongalba.

I think children should be taught now because they are the men and women of tomorrow... It's the children who are going to change the world for the better, not the adults.

When the children come to Moongalba I teach them the same as I teach my own grandchildren. I teach them how to pick up shellfish and how to look for them. I teach them how to fish and to crab. I teach them what's good to eat in the bush and what isn't, and I teach them how to cook food under the ground.[4]

Moongalba also welcomed trainee teachers, as well as tertiary students of Anthropology, Architecture, Black Studies and Environmental Studies. The visitors' book also recorded the names of distinguished writers, artists, dancers, educators, MPs – and Spike Milligan.

Visiting academics were regular callers – from around Australia, certainly, and also from the United States, Japan, Germany, the USSR, Nigeria, Sweden and various Pacific islands. Their interest in the project meant Kath received many formal invitations to visit other countries.

As a result she was able to incorporate information about other cultures in her Moongalba teaching with some hands-on activities.

Having travelled all over the world, I've picked up a bit of art from each of the countries and taken them home and the kids can sit there and communicate through touch with these artifacts. One mother asked me if I was afraid the children would break them. I told her that if they do I'll go back to that particular country and get another one! What the heck! Children are losing a very important part of growing up by having to go to museums and look at things through glass... and nothing has been broken at Moongalba.[5]

With Moongalba so well established as a centre for disseminating knowledge and respect for Aboriginal culture, Kath had good reason to expect that her request for legal tenure of the land would be granted. In early 1973 she asked Gordon Bryant, Minister for Aboriginal Affairs in the Whitlam administration, to negotiate with the Redland Shire Council and the Queensland government. She explained that she could not accept the Council's conditions in the lease and that she would make another submission. Promises of support, including substantial financial help, did indeed come from the Whitlam government, on the proviso that the Queensland government agreed; but, with Bjelke-Petersen as premier, there was little chance of that.

Should a more permanent occupancy have been granted, Kath was ready to begin construction. She had approached various architects and had a blueprint of a "revolutionary design [which was] inexpensive to construct". She was not about to give up now, knockback or no. Moongalba was already a centre for learning and cultural exchange and Kath wanted to realise the entire project. As well as the enthusiastic support of the Aborigines living at Dunwich and One Mile, she had the moral support and the promise of financial assistance from many influential people in the white community, among them Manfred Cross and the writers Judith Wright McKinney, Nancy Cato and Rodney Hall. She also met Dr H.C. Coombs, former governor of the Commonwealth (later Reserve) Bank, who was convinced that money spent on Moongalba was money well spent. (Later, in 1979, he was chairman of the Aboriginal Treaty Committee and Judith Wright was one of its eight members – the treaty that never happened.) In an ABC Radio speech on 2 June 1979 Dr Coombs said:

> In taking the land we did not merely deprive Aborigines of property. We took also the source of their livelihood, the very foundation of their society, the basis of the rights and obligations on which it was built, and above all the source of the religious convictions which gave purpose and justification to their lives.[6]

There was no shortage of willing volunteers to help make Moongalba a permanent place for celebrating Aboriginal culture and informing people of its importance in the world. Architecture students drew up designs of buildings for permanent use, electricity was connected, a Swedish composting toilet was installed and the grounds and temporary buildings carefully maintained.

Judith Wright was a most energetic and enthusiastic supporter from the outset. She wrote:

> [Moongalba] is a fine way to learn about other people – a kind of painless education that leaves happy memories and can change bad attitudes and prejudices forever.
>
> It is also a place to bring sorrows and problems. Kath is well-versed in the difficulties Aborigines have with white officialdom, in getting such rights as are theirs and in knowing how to go about it. Personal problems come to her, too, and often the talk goes on most of the night.
>
> But above all, Moongalba is a place to relax, away from the hostile and critical eyes of white people, in a place Aborigines can feel is their own. The far-off lights of Brisbane are muted by the trees, and people can be themselves, acting out their real lives, singing their own songs, laughing and dancing, miming and learning, and talking freely.
>
> It is a place, too, where white people can begin to understand as they never otherwise could, what it is to be Aboriginal.[7]

The bond between the women strengthened when Kath stayed with

Judith in the summer of 1971/72 at Mt Tamborine, near Brisbane. Kath was then writing *Stradbroke Dreamtime* and Judith now wrote her poem "Two Dreamtimes" for her (the poem appears on p. 206). Though she is one of the conquerors and Kath one of the persecuted, both have shared "sad tales of women/(black or white at a different price)". "We are shadow sisters," she writes, and symbolically offers Kath a weapon shaped by the conquerors.

Kath often said that she was so moved by the poem that she was unable to read it aloud for many months; and it was three years before she felt able to reply in kind: "Sister poet, I answer you," she began.

The two friends came together again to make a film about Moongalba; *Shadow Sisters* was first shown in Sydney in July 1977. Having met Judith at the ferry, Kath shows her around Moongalba against nature's gentle background music of wind in the trees, birds flying overhead, and the gentle jingling of Kath's seashell curtains. Kath speaks of the Aboriginal children who live on the fringes of the white man's cities, cut off from the privileges of white children and alienated from knowledge of their own culture. She explains how Moongalba restores to these children a knowledge of their history and a pride in their identity.

They learnt to respect the environment and their Aboriginal ancestors' traditional lifestyle... Often, it was the first time in their lives they heard and saw something of the rich culture of their heritage.[8]

She takes some children to collect sea creatures for a meal and launches a small boat into the water. They help to prepare a *kup-mari* – a feast at which the meat, wrapped in banana leaves, cooks for hours in a slow earthen oven.

The film was produced by Frank Heimans, and Kath won an international acting award for her role in it, as well as membership of the Black Hall of Fame. It is compelling visual testimony in support of Judith Wright's assertion that Moongalba

 [w]hether officials approve of it or not... is there, and functioning in pride and dignity. If white apathy and ungenerosity won't support it, it will still be real, the living achievement of a woman who is Stradbroke

Sister Poet

Sister poet, I answer you,
Where you sit with your "civilised" kin
Shadow sister, your high ideals
Compensate me for their sin.

Today you fight for Fraser,
Armed with document and pen.
You the embarrassing "stirrer"
Scorned by "civilised" men.

You, the protector of Nature's Hearth,
Attacking greed and corruption
And those who make their living
Raping the bowels of Mother Earth.

Roaming east, north, south, and west,
You talk and write and hope and pray,
That in your lifetime's call,
Man will respect and protect
Nature's balance realm
That was created for all.

My shadow sister, I talk to you,
From my sit down place with the Koori dead.
In Quandamooka the knife I threw
I know not where the handle lies.

But, my shadow sister, this I know,
Your dreams are my dreams
Your thoughts are my thoughts
And our shadow that made us sisters
That binds us close together,
Together with us
CRIES…

Island's...most famous daughter and citizen. More may come of it than any white officialdom could ever give, or would ever conceive of giving.[9]

Much *has* come of it. The thousands of children who passed through Moongalba are now adults, the student teachers are now teachers – people who help forge links of proper understanding between two cultures.

Burr-Nong
(BORA RING)

The time of learning in the Aboriginal world never stops. It goes on and on. As soon as the children are able to sit up, they are taught to observe the reptiles, animals and birds and to draw them in the sand. In this way they learn to recognise every creature of the bush. And they learn, too, how to imitate their calls and cries.

The most exciting period of learning comes when the children are about twelve years old. At this time they learn the lessons from within the Burr-Nong ring. It is a period of testing, and they go on with it until they have passed every test – when they are between sixteen and eighteen. After they have passed out of the Burr-Nong, they are called men and women of the tribe.

During the Burr-Nong training the boys are handed over to the men of the tribe, and the girls to the women. They are taught the tribal secrets, and the art of manhood and womanhood...

The boys are taught the tribal legends and must learn them by heart; for the Aborigines had no written language, and could not record their stories except in their hearts and minds. The children are also taught patience and tolerance, and the art of pain-bearing. No child is allowed to think of himself as being cleverer than another. If any child boasts of his ability during the Burr-Nong training, he would be severely punished by the tribal elders. No child is more important than another; they must all help each other to pass the tests.[10]

With the move to Moongalba, Kath abandoned wearing conventional Western clothes in favour of long, flowing, Asian-style garments.

MOONGALBA • 99

Visiting American professor Margaret Read Lauer wrote about the "three and a half unforgettable days" she spent at Moongalba. In an article for the journal, *World Literature Written in English*, she presents a personal appreciation of Kath's work, her philosophy and her Aboriginality.[11] She describes her last evening with Kath when, "full of good seafood and wine, and having put off as long as possible this formality of interview with question-and-answer limitations, Kath and I set ourselves to the task. It went somewhat better than either of us had anticipated." Extracts from the interview follow.

Moongalba could be a place of escape, an ivory tower kind of place for a poet. It's anything but that. Does it represent... another kind of concept but one related to your particular idea of a poet?

When I came here I didn't escape society because society came to me. When I was working in the civil rights movement...I always yearned for a place to come and recharge my batteries, to bide-a-wee, and then go back to society renewed and ready to work again. Moongalba is a place where leaders and potential leaders can come, a sitting-down place to recover physical and spiritual health and to return to society the best they have to offer; a place where they can become rejuvenated in order to keep fighting for the good of mankind.

I think my poetry, since I came here, has changed, is now more subtle. I now fight for butcher birds, for university students, for the rights of possums, for everything that is alive, not just the human race, but everything – be they plants, snakes or golden orb spiders – because man is lost without any of these. Man has the power to communicate but has fallen down on the job.

Why is it so important to you to work with children?

Because the children are the ones who will create the change. You must learn things at a very tender age. It's the children who are innocent and ready to learn. It's the children who are the hope of mankind. And frankly I am tired of talking to mentally constipated adults... Children don't have racist attitudes unless they're taught by adults.

Do you think that poets and children are especially close?

Children and artists, any creative artists, are close. Children are very creative people and they stay that way until they join the establishment...

Do you think being a woman, especially an Aboriginal woman, changes or determines the definition of a poet?

No. It has nothing to do with sex. I think that women poets have a more logical and yet very heavy emotional impact because woman is the seed carrier and it is through women that the next generation comes. But this we cannot achieve without men.

Does [being a poet] mean special obligations? Does it mean relief from social responsibility?

Poets are born, but they are not born poets. Society creates the system that the poet is born into, and the poet has to work at becoming a poet through this system. Through poetry, the poet tries to bring about change in the society. Poets are teachers of change, critics of society. The poet is but a tool of society – not the yes-man but the camera that exposes the good and the bad of society.

It seems astonishing that local, state and federal governments continued to deny Kath legal title to the land she was using for the benefit of so many people. No doubt the personal prejudices – and the personal power – of the Queensland premier, Joh Bjelke-Petersen, were a key factor, as they were in the continuing refusal to allow the claims of Eddie Mabo. When, in 1983, Kath made a second attempt to enter state Parliament (this time for the Democrats) she sheeted home the blame to the state government, as the *Courier-Mail* reported:

> The Government was blocking plans for an Aboriginal Cultural Centre and Museum on Stradbroke Island out of political spite, Aboriginal poet

Mrs Kath Walker said yesterday.

Mrs Walker, the Democrat candidate for the Redland electorate, said the Federal Aboriginal Development Commission had offered $250,000 to finance the building but this can't be paid over because the Queensland Government won't let the Stradbroke Aborigines have a secure base lease on the site.[12]

In 1979 Kath prepared a submission to the federal Department of Aboriginal Affairs. She had the assistance of Julianne Schwenke, a postgraduate student who was hoping to write a scholarly biography of Kath. The lengthy document defines the past and present status of the land, describes amenities provided through the work of volunteers, and outlines in detail developmental plans for the future.

A board of management was then in the process of being set up by Aboriginal Legal Aid solicitors. Five of the eight board members belonged to the local Aboriginal community, one was a Maori and two were white women. Kath was the managing director of Moongalba—The Noonuccal–Nughie Educational Centre—and Julianne Schwenke its secretary.

Perhaps of greater significance is the modest sum requested as financial assistance. The submission asks for an initial grant of $10,000, a small sum, considering the scope of the enterprise envisaged. It is stated that voluntary work and generous financial contributions, which had already enabled much to be done at Moongalba, would continue to assist the development. The availability of plans and specifications by University of Queensland Architect James MacCormack is mentioned, as is the willingness of donors to subscribe to Moongalba:

> During the last six years, Mrs Walker has donated all her income as a best-selling author to the project. Individuals such as Judith Wright have donated thousands of dollars and many thousands of hours of labour.

The submission concludes with the following:

> The board appreciates the Department's reluctance to fund a project where the land title is not guaranteed. We therefore respectfully request the Department's aid in securing the land for the Noonuccal–Nughie people of Stradbroke Island, and look forward to financial aid when the land is returned to its traditional owners.[13]

It was grossly unjust that this application, reasonable in its demands and with well-supported arguments, received no response, but such was the case.

How much did the knockbacks really matter? In a sense they mattered greatly because a worthwhile enterprise was improperly thwarted and because a woman whose initiatives and enormous talents were acclaimed around the world was denied practical recognition by governments in a country that was hers much more than it was theirs. Yet, in another sense, they did not matter too much because Kath made Moongalba work in spite of them.

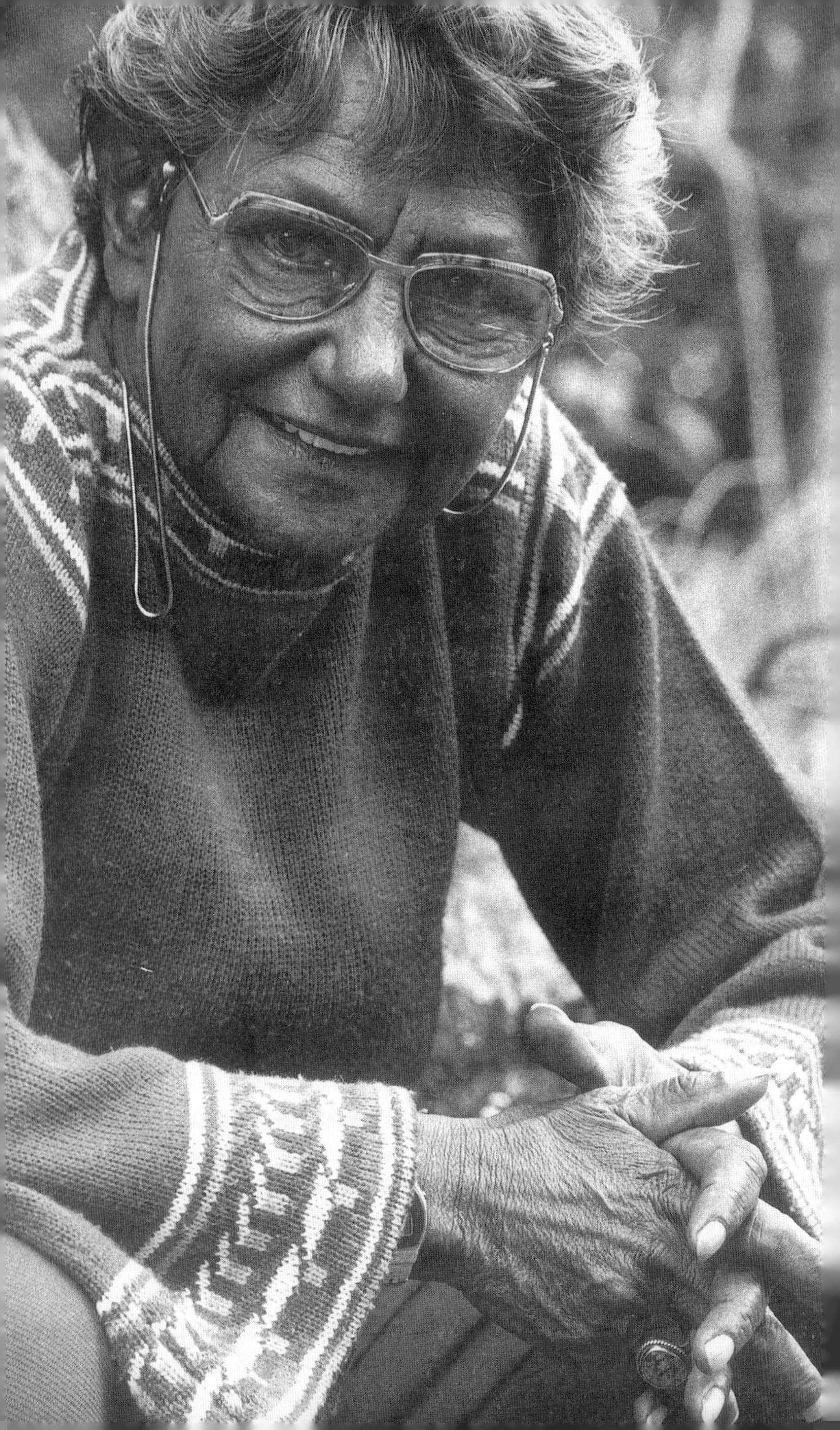

Acclaim

As Kath's reputation as a poet and as a civil rights activist spread in the seventies, invitations came from all quarters of the globe. But, thanks to good planning, the progress of the Moongalba project was not put on hold when she was away. Helpers managed to keep things going in Kath's absence and she even came home to diaries that detailed daily progress.

In 1972, the year *Stradbroke Dreamtime* was published, she was invited to tour and lecture in New Zealand. While there, she agreed to be a guest lecturer at the University of the South Pacific in Fiji early the next year. Within twelve months she was Australia's official envoy at the International Writers' Conference (Hari Sasra) in Malaysia; and she also flew to Nigeria with another Aboriginal Australian, John Moriarty, and Chris McGuigan, adviser to the Aboriginal Council for the Arts. These three were members of a steering committee for the Second World Black and African Festival of Arts and Culture. Their brief was to plan Australia's contribution to the festival. On the return trip Kath was caught up in a life or death situation which, at the time, drove all thought of meetings and agendas from her mind. It was an event that made news all over the world.

The BOAC plane on which the three Australians were travelling landed in Dubai on 21 November 1974 after a long flight from Beirut.[1] Wanting to stretch their legs, John Moriarty and Chris McGuigan disembarked, but Kath remained on board, hoping to catch up on some sleep. Hers was a fated choice: she would not see her companions again for the rest of the journey.

Commonplace

The rat-tat-tat of rifles
Bombards my sleep.
Bolted door shuts out commonplace.
Pointed revolver sharpens my senses
And I move automatically
Down the aisle of the DC 10.
Sit, obey, keep calm
The blinds shut out the landscape.
The DC 10 pants on hot desert sands
Like a wounded eagle,
Ever alert to any change
That might come
To blow strength into her wings.
The DC 10 waits,
Recovering her breath,
Waiting for embassies to negotiate
Tired aching flesh of humankind.
Exchange the cargoes;
It is done.
The giant DC 10 bird
Shudders from her long hot rest.
Her engines vibrate her intention
As she turns her majestic steel frame
And like the eagle flies
With her melting drooping cargo
Back to commonplace.

Sleep came to her peacefully, but she woke up to find herself staring down the barrel of an automatic revolver. "Is this a hijack?" she asked.

The tall black man held the gun in his right hand and with his left clasped the arm of the chief steward, who begged Kath to do as she was told. The hijacker was moving the forty or so passengers who remained on board to a middle section of Economy class, while two other men moved along the aisles with their repeating rifles. Suddenly gunfire erupted outside the plane, and a caterer and a flight attendant returning to the hijacked aircraft were injured.

By now Kath and the other passengers realised that their hijackers were Arabs. One who spoke English interrogated Kath, asking her if she was Indian or Pakistani. He looked astonished when she told him she was an Aboriginal Australian. She said that she was sympathetic to the Arab cause but believed actions such as this would not further it; that he and his associates would be better employed working for the World Black Festival of Arts that was to take place in Nigeria soon. The young man was not angered by her comments and about five hours later, when the plane was airborne, she learned that he worked for the airport catering service in Dubai and had been abducted to serve as an interpreter.

The hijackers' purpose was to gain the release of two Palestinian prisoners in Holland and thirteen in Egypt. In the early hours of 22 November the hijacked plane landed at Tripoli and the captain informed passengers that they were awaiting a French correspondent who would negotiate with the hijackers for the release of the prisoners in Egypt. After half a day of waiting – rations were down to two biscuits and a small cup of water every two hours – the hijackers gave up waiting.

The plane flew on to Tunis and, once more, waited. The window blinds were pulled down but the heat was terrible. It was now 23 November and the hijackers had presumably decided that some further act of terrorism was needed. After going along the aisle asking passengers their nationality, they selected a German and took him to the back of the plane. Two shots rang out, the external stairs were lowered, and the body was rolled out.

The French had proved recalcitrant to negotiations in Tripoli but the authorities in Tunis were much more amenable. They agreed to make contact with the Dutch authorities and within a few hours the two prisoners in Holland had been flown to Tunis. Some hard bargaining now followed between the hijackers and the Egyptian authorities, with the Tunisians in the role of humanitarian go-betweens: they bargained with the Egyptians for a fair trial in Cairo for the hijackers if they surrendered immediately and let the passengers go free.

The hijackers did agree to release some hostages, those with Indian, Pakistani and Malaysian passports, but not holders of British passports. Kath, with her Australian passport, was classed as British! However, in a second wave of releases, women with British passports were freed – and Kath. They took back their passports and gathered their bags, then slid down a rope until their feet came to a ladder propped against the plane. The vehicle that transported the women away from the airport was a Black Maria, the irony of which was not lost on Kath: part of the system used to keep Aborigines firmly under white control, here she was now being rescued in one – and, what is more, being told to lie on the floor for safety. At the Hilton Hotel in Tunis an entire floor had been taken over by BOAC. A group of doctors and ancillary medical staff checked the health of the women and Kath was invited to use the phone to ring anywhere in the world. Within minutes she was speaking to her sister Florrie on Stradbroke Island. Florrie received the call with incredulous joy and Kath told her to tell their sister Lucy as soon as possible.

Lucy worked in the laundry at Princess Alexandra Hospital in Brisbane, and Florrie thought it would be better to tell her in person rather than to leave a phone message. So she caught the ferry – a fifty minute journey across Moreton Bay – and then set out on the long bus-ride from Cleveland to Brisbane. When Lucy caught sight of Florrie at the end of a long corridor, she cried out: "She's dead, she's dead" and fell to the floor in a faint.

The hijacking and its vicissitudes were watched by the media around the world, and updates were broadcast as news came to hand. When Kath eventually arrived home, the cameras were waiting and her weary face spoke about the ordeal.

Yussef
(Hijacker)

Yussef, my son,
What do you do here,
With your dreamy eyes
That tell of moonlight
And sun
And the warm soft touch
Of a girl's embrace?
The love you feel for children
Pours out of your heart
And it's easy to see
Since you wear it on your sleeve.
The soft lines around your mouth
Tell of endearments
You dare not speak.
Your tired eyes
Have seen blood and tears
Fear and contempt.
I see you in the moonlight
Relaxing,
Contented in a girl's embrace.
But reality clouds my vision;
For there you stand,
Erect,
Alert,
Caressing
A repeating rifle
In your desert-strong
Sunburned hands.

It was typical of Kath that she had the composure to write poetry in the midst of the drama on the plane. The air-sickness bag in the pocket in front of her was the only paper to be had, so she made do with that. She had found out that Yussef, the leader of the terrorists, had sacrificed his career as a pediatrician for the life of a terrorist. In one poem she wondered how a world could have gone so wrong that a young man would throw away his stethoscope and pick up a rifle.

Kath kept the two poems she wrote on the unlikely stationery but did not publish them, and she was unable to find them when I asked her to let me see them. It was a happy day when I discovered they had turned up among her papers in the Fryer Library.

The Lagos festival had special importance for Australia and its indigenous people. Before Kath and her two compatriots set out for the 1974 steering committee meeting, Prime Minister Gough Whitlam had officially sanctioned Australia's participation and had approved the allocation of substantial funds to cover preparation and transport costs. A report presented by Kath, John Moriarty and Chris McGuigan stated:

> The Black community of Australia regards the participation in the Second World Black and African Festival of Arts and Culture as an extremely important step in forging an Aboriginal identity. This will be the first occasion on which Australia has been represented at an international event by an all Black delegation.[2]

There were to be several hiccups before the Lagos festival became a reality. Internal political upheavals in Nigeria caused two postponements but it did eventually take place and was a huge success, from the opening ceremony on 15 January 1977 until it closed a month later. Kath was proud to be there as an Australian delegate and senior adviser to the festival; and she was delighted at the extent and variety of the exhibitions and activities. There was dancing, singing, ceremonial costume,

Kath received an Oscar Micheaux award for the film *Shadow Sister* at the sixth annual awards presentation of the Black Filmmakers' Hall of Fame in Oakland, California in February 1979. With her are actor/singer Lena Horne and Vivian.

With American actor, Paul Winfield, Oakland, California, 1979

sculpture, mask-making, craft, drama and a magnificent display of artifacts from many black cultures. She found it altogether satisfying. And her return home, this time, was uneventful.

In 1975 she attended the Papua New Guinea Festival of Arts as a guest of the government and three years later she went to the United States as poet in residence at Bloomsburg State College, Pennsylvania. She had won a Fulbright Scholarship and a Myer Travel Grant which enabled her to make the journey. From there she was invited to visit and lecture at a number of other campuses. In the four months from November 1978 to February 1979 she visited Lock Haven State College, Pennsylvania; Concorde University, Montreal; the Institute of American Indian Arts at Santa Fe, New Mexico; and the University of California, Berkeley.

As I have travelled throughout the world, I have often thought that one could judge a society by the way it treats its racial minorities. Where a minority was forced to live in squalor, I have seen a squalid society. Where a minority was riddled with disease, I have seen a sick society. Where a minority was without hope, I saw a nation without hope.[3]

Kath turned sixty in 1980 and Channel 7 in Brisbane organised a *This Is Your Life* programme for her. The show's American producer, Helen Ives, rang me to ask if I would agree to appear on the show. Everyone kept the secret and the surprise for Kath was enhanced by the travel arrangements. Compere Roger Climpson flew to Stradbroke Island on the pretext that he was to discuss with her her interest in conservation. Dramatically he announced that she was to fly back to Brisbane with him in the Channel 7 helicopter to appear on *This Is Your Life*. The outfit she wore on the show had been smuggled out of Moongalba by one of her relations and was waiting for her at the studio.

Helen Ives had invited an array of guests who between them provided a broad coverage of Kath's busy life. There was Ruby Robinson, who for many years had been the *Courier-Mail* reporter on women's sports and who reminisced about Kath's abilities as a player of vigoro and cricko; and Phyllis Manson who had captained the cricko team that had been so successful. Eris Valentine reminded her of their days in AWAS together.

Alastair Campbell, Faith Bandler and I congratulated her on her contribution to the Aboriginal rights movement. Rodney Hall reminded her of her association with the Realist Writers. An old friend from Melbourne, Merle Jacomos, who was involved in the Victorian Aboriginal rights movement, said she had brought a message from all the Koories in Victoria: "Kath, we loves yer".

Flown out specially from Britain was Peter Woodford, chief steward on the hijacked plane. He recalled how he and Kath had worked together to keep up the morale of the other hostages. "Remember how we got the people singing?" he said. "You were an inspiration to us all." Then there was John Moriarty, who had escaped the hijack because he had disembarked to stretch his legs.

ABOVE: Unexpected reunion with the chief steward of the hijacked BOAC plane, Peter Woodford, in 1980. "Remember how we got the people singing?" he said.

LEFT: Fond sisters, Kath and Lucy. Lucy has lived in Brisbane since she married but she loves to return to the island to go fishing. Her affection and admiration for Kath was unbounded.

ABOVE: With Kath on stage on *This Is Your Life* are daughter-in-law Patty Walker, grandchildren Che, Petrina, Joshua and Raymond, and teenager Leroy Hart who "adopted" Patty's family.

RIGHT: Eris Valentine, Kath's friend from their days together in AWAS

ACCLAIM • 115

Don Dunstan sent a message on videotape reminding Kath of their trip to London for the World Council of Churches and of their mutual concern with civil rights for Aborigines; and a telegram from Judith Wright expressed affection and admiration. Jacaranda Press was represented by Col Cunnington, who reminded Kath how her first manuscript had arrived with a letter of recommendation from Judith. He had the precious manuscript with him and presented it to her. Poet Jack Davis said he thought so highly of her poems that he read them more often than he read his own. Story-teller Percy Tresize and artist Dick Roughsey said how important it was for them as Aborigines to employ artistic means to convey their messages to the world.

There were members of her family, so special a part of her life – her sister Lucy, her grandchildren and, to her enormous surprise and delight, her son Vivian, whom Channel Seven had flown out from America, where he ran a nightclub.

The following year another honour almost came Kath's way. Queensland observes the quaint custom of celebrating Queensland Day each year on 6 June in remembrance of the separation of the colony from New South Wales in 1859. Premier Joh Bjelke-Petersen encouraged the annual selection of a "Queenslander of the Year", on whom the honour was conferred on Queensland Day. In 1981 Kath was nominated, and the voting results placed her among the six finalists. Despite some reservations about the award, she felt it was quite good for an Aborigine to be a finalist. As it happened she was not selected from the shortlist but could vouch for the winner – her friend and former employer, Lady Cilento. In 1985 Kath won the Australian title, Aboriginal of the Year.

Father Son and Mother Earth was a small publication for children about the environmental wastage of Stradbroke caused particularly by sandminers and developers. Kath wrote it and illustrated it, and

Jacaranda published it in 1981. Her friend and publisher at Jacaranda, John Collins, recalled her work:

> In her little private time at Moongalba Kath had begun to sketch and paint. Just as the text for the story combined the Aboriginal view of creation with the all too modern era of destruction, so her sketches were a similar fusion of old and new. The only problem was the medium. This was solved when the Jacaranda art department found a decently spare box of felt-tipped pens. So a remarkably unique style emerged…[4]

Another publication that year was *My People*, a collection of previously published poems. Kath had written no new poems for publication for over a decade, and believed her days of poetry writing were over. Fortunately she was wrong.

In September/October 1984, she was one of a five member cultural delegation to China. Historian Manning Clark, one of her companions, wrote of her:

> China worked a great miracle in her. She had not written any poetry for years. Within forty-eight hours of arriving in Shanghai a light began to shine in her eyes. She began to sparkle: she bubbled with excitement. I remember the morning she said to me with an engaging twinkle in her eye, "Manning, I'm pregnant again." She meant she had started to write poems again.[5]

The poems from China were published in both English and Chinese, each poem in English accompanied by its Chinese translation. They were written in China, at a time when Chinese people were feeling particularly optimistic about their future. The anti-academic influence of the so-called Cultural Revolution was over, and schools and universities had re-opened and were encouraging international contacts. English had long replaced Russian as the preferred second language for Chinese students. The Australian delegation was one of many groups then touring the country and experiencing the warmth of Chinese interest them and the enthusiasm of the belief that a better future beckoned.

Reed Flute Cave

I didn't expect to meet you in Guilin
My Rainbow Serpent,
My Earth Mother,
But you were there
In Reed Flute Cave,
With animals and reptiles
And all those things
You stored in the Dreamtime.
Pools of cool water, like mirrors,
Reflecting your underbelly.

The underground storage place,
Where frogs store water in their stomachs
And mushrooms and every type of fruit,
Vegetable, animal and fish,
Are on display.

Perhaps I have strayed too long
In this beautiful country;
The reed flutes are playing a mournful tune.
The cool air rushing through
The rock cathedral
Reminds me of the sea breezes
Of Stradbroke
And the reed flute seems
To be capturing the scene.
The slippery earth stone floor
Takes me back to mud sea flats,
Where seaweeds communicate with oysters
Fish and crabs.
Have you travelled all this way
To remind me to return home?

Kath and Manning Clark against a spectacular backdrop near Guilin

OPPOSITE:
Members of the 1984 cultural delegation to China in Guangzhou: from left, Eric Tan (W.A.); Robert Adams (Australian Council of Arts); Kath Walker; the Australian consul-general in China; Caroline Turner (leader of delegation); Manning Clark; Mr Fu (interpreter)

Uluru, your resting place in Australia,
Will not be the same without you.

I shall return home,
But I'm glad I came.
Tell me, my Rainbow Spirit,
Was there just one of you?
Perhaps, now I have time to think,
Perhaps, you are but one of many guardians
Of earth's peoples,
Just one,
My Rainbow Serpent,
Spirit of my Mother Earth.

Kath Walker in China was published under an arrangement between the International Culture Publishing Corporation of Beijing and Jacaranda Press. Although the year of publication was 1988, printing and binding in China was slow and stock did not arrive in Brisbane until late 1989. In the meantime the slaughter in Tienanmen Square had occurred, in June, shocking the world.

On her visit to Beijing, Kath had written a short poem about Tienanmen Square, which began:

The big square
Welcomes
Her sons and daughters
And visitors alike.

When stock of the book finally arrived in Brisbane, she at first refused to allow it to be released. In the end a new dust jacket for the Australian edition was designed and Kath, persuaded by Vivian, relented. She wrote a "Requiem" which appeared on the back:

In Tienanmen Square
History repeats itself.
Man's lust for power
Rises through
The smoke-filled air.

One Saturday in 1986 Kath phoned John Collins.

"I'm ringing you from the post office at Dunwich."
"Why?"
"I've just collected a yard of telex. It's the longest I've ever seen."
"Where is it from?"
"Moscow."
"Who signed it?"
"A fella called Gorbachev!"[6]

Oodgeroo with friends Rita Moriarty, Dick Roughsey, and John Moriarty

It was an invitation to attend the International Forum for a Nuclear-Free World for the Survival of Humanity. Kath felt honoured to be asked and hoped that her humanist/conservationist beliefs would be a positive contribution. However, she was disillusioned when she arrived in Moscow to find the conference overwhelmingly dominated by scientists, among whom there was little sign of openness. Perhaps the seeds of discord that were to wreck the Soviet Union were already showing signs of germination. Although she felt she could have made a reasonable contribution to the conference she was not given any real opportunity. On the return to Australia she stopped over at New Delhi to deliver a lecture on "Aboriginal Grassroots Culture".

Oodgeroo in her screen role as the witch-like Ole Eva in Bruce Beresford's film *The Fringe Dwellers*.

At home academic honours were heaped upon her. She received the degree of Honorary Doctorate of Letters from Macquarie University (1988), Griffith University (1989), Monash University (1991) and Queensland University of Technology (1992). Clearly she was undaunted by the ceremonial formalities of academia, for the acceptance speeches she made on these occasions lack none of her customary fire. Some of these speeches are collected in Part Three of this book.

Film producer Bruce Beresford offered Kath something new in 1986 when he invited her to be a script consultant on *The Fringe Dwellers*, a movie he was making based on the novel by Nene Gare. This involvement was exciting, especially when Kath was assigned the character role of a frightening, witch-like old woman. With the help of stage make-up and an atrocious wig, she ended up looking the part.

Much to Kath's delight, the performing arts were soon to make another claim upon her. The Queensland State and Municipal Choir commissioned Australian-born composer Malcolm Williamson, Master of the Queen's Music, to write a work for them to perform in 1988, the year of the Australian bicentenary. The choir suggested that he use Australian poetry as his text and gave him Kath's books to peruse. He was keen to use *The Dawn Is At Hand* and approached Oodgeroo (as she was now called) for permission.

The composition, unfortunately, was not ready on time, but the work was eventually performed in October 1989; Dobbs Franks conducted the Queensland Symphony Orchestra and Queensland State and Municipal Choir in the Concert Hall of the Performing Arts Complex in Brisbane. Oodgeroo invited Bob and me to join her and Vivian and other guests at the performance. The composer was also present. He had arrived just in time – punctuality obviously not a strong point – wearing a knitted vest with a design of the Aboriginal flag on it. At interval I told him I liked it. "You do?" he said. "So does the Queen."

A UK edition of *The Dawn Is At Hand* was published in 1992; in the Foreword Malcolm Williamson wrote about "the mercurial personality of the poet who could recite poems, mostly not of her own but which she admired, interposed with bawdy anecdotes [and] mercilessly accurate denunciations of those who deserved them".[7]

The arts world's final tribute in Oodgeroo's lifetime was to come in 1993 with the Queensland Theatre Company's play, *One Woman's Song*, by Peta Murray, which was based on her early life.

At the post-concert supper following the first performance of Malcolm Williamson's oratorio *The Dawn Is At Hand* in 1989 are, front row from left, conductor Dobbs Franks; Oodgeroo; Malcolm Williamson; Kevin Power, director of the Queensland State and Municipal Choir.

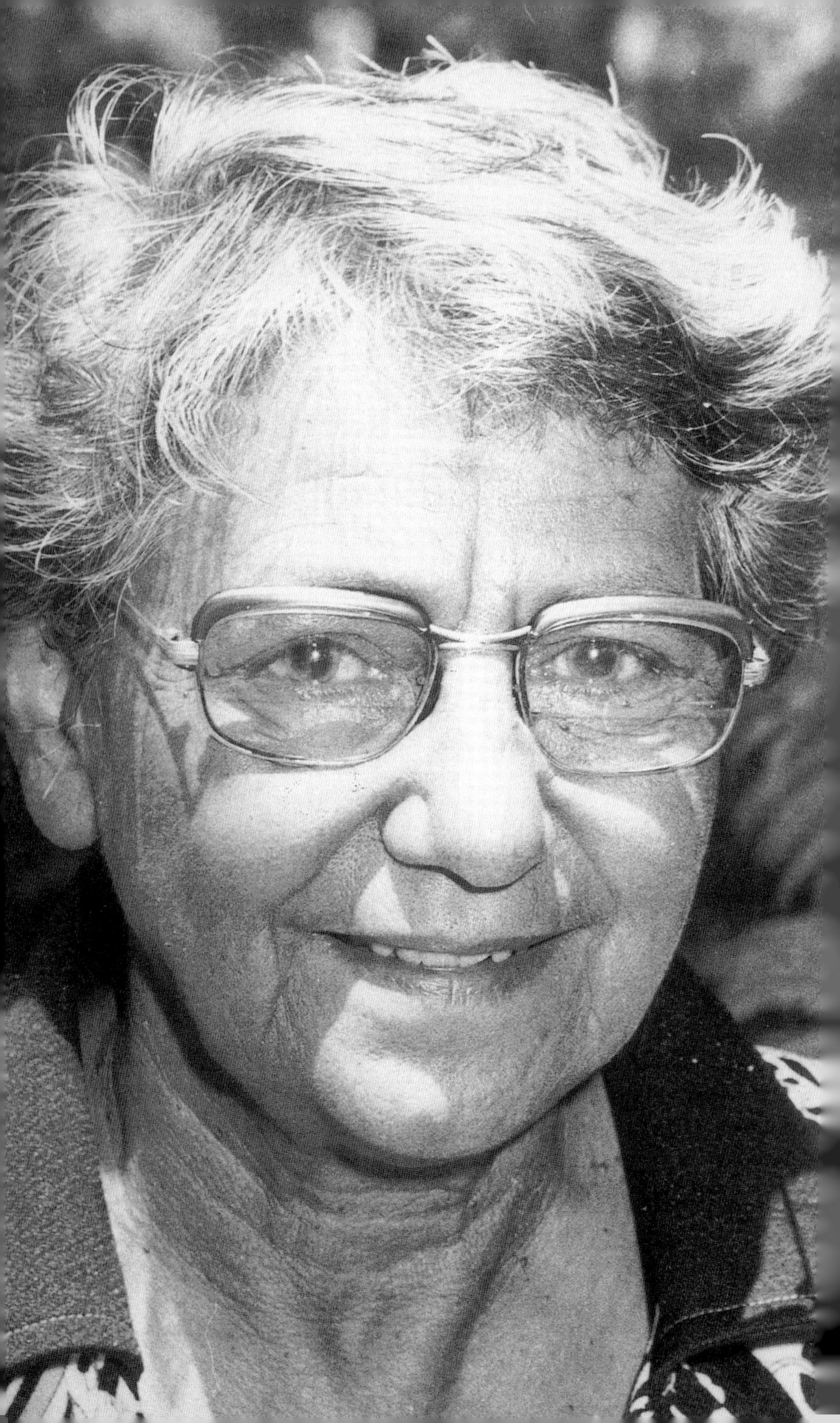

Oodgeroo

White Australians believed they were honouring the two-hundredth anniversary of the birth of a new nation, now a pleasant, happy country for most to live in; but not many of them had much of an idea about what the beginning was really like. In *The Fatal Shore*, a history of convict Australia, Robert Hughes writes:

> No other country had such a birth, and its pangs can be said to have begun on the afternoon of January 26, 1788, when a fleet of eleven vessels carrying 1,030 people, including 548 male and 188 female convicts, under the command of Captain Arthur Phillip in his flagship Sirius, entered Port Jackson.[1]

He continues: "One may liken this moment to the breaking open of a capsule." A time capsule, indeed, of formidable proportions!

> Upon the harbor the ships were now entering, European history had left no mark at all. Until the swollen sails and curvetting bows of the British fleet came round South Head, there were no dates. The Aborigines and the fauna around them had possessed the landscape since time immemorial, and no other human eye had seen them. Now the protective glass of distance broke in an instant, never to be restored.[2]

There were no dates. This was a timeless land. According to the British Colonial Office, there were no people either – none, at least, of any account.

There were many reasons why the colonists considered Aboriginal people to be lesser creatures than apes. There were the obvious things, like our nakedness and different standards of physical beauty, but there was also their greed-based refusal to give credence to and therefore comprehend a non European-earth-raping culture, which, through an ancient excellence in social engineering, was not only highly successful but superior to their own.

We "pagans", who had believed in and comfortably maintained our own strict "code of moral behaviour" for all of our people for many thousands of years before the white man's culture was born, were soon to learn that the equivalent order, in their brave new world, was most sadistically maintained with the rabid and obsessive use of the infamous cat-o'-nine-tails whip.[3]

When James Cook and Joseph Banks returned to England after the 1770 voyage, they reported that the southern land whose east coast they had discovered and explored was a land that belonged to no one – a *terra nullius*. There had been a number of encounters between the indigenous people and the crew of the *Endeavour*, but to eighteenth-century Europeans, nomadic hunter–gatherers had no legal claim to the land that supported them—an outrageous idea today. We now know that Aborigines regarded themselves as custodians of the land; we know that each group had responsibility for a well-defined territory which outsiders might not enter without their permission; and we know that they inhabited the entire continent for at least forty thousand years.

The descendants of these people could hardly be expected to join in celebrations commemorating the arrival of white Europeans who usurped them, murdered them, ruthlessly cleared the land and introduced destructive, hard-hoofed animals. How could it have been expected that Aboriginal people would allow this celebration by the white invaders of the "glorious" achievements of their forefathers' conquest to take place without comment? Would this not have been a reaffirmation of *terra nullius*?

Two hundred years had gone by with no treaty, no recognition of the need for restitution. Kath Walker felt that as an Aborigine with an international reputation she should make some significant gesture. In 1987 John Collins received another phonecall from Stradbroke Island. It was Kath, from Moongalba. She had been awarded an MBE in 1970.

"Will you come with me to Government House?"
"Whatever for?"
"To hand back that medal…"

We journeyed up Fernberg Road and crunched our way across the gravel of the vice-regal establishment. The governor's secretary met us and, over a very polite but also very understanding cup of coffee, the MBE

John Collins...
publisher, mentor,
friend

was handed over. As we drove away, Kath said: "I don't know whether it will make much difference but I certainly feel better."[4]

Now that the plans for the bicentennial celebrations were an insult to the descendants of Aboriginal Australia, she felt she should not be in receipt of a British honour while her people were being dishonoured.

Her next decision was to abandon her English-derived name, Walker. Very few eastern Aborigines had preserved their tribal names, and Kath knew only that she was most certainly of the North Stradbroke people called Noonuccal. So she chose an Aboriginal word for the paperbark tree and called herself Oodgeroo of the Noonuccal people.

An Aboriginal friend protested: "But Kath, you're famous as Kath Walker," to which the newly self-named Oodgeroo replied: "Well, I'll just have to start all over again and get famous as Oodgeroo." The gesture was mainly intended for white Australians, and it was readily accepted by those who already admired her achievements.

The descendants of the white invaders were about to have a great festival to celebrate their conquest, and Oodgeroo wondered how the Aboriginal people would respond. There were many among them now who were aware of their own sad history and no longer willing to remain passive victims. It was an awareness she herself had helped to build over the last thirty years.

Paperbark Tree

In the new Dreamtime there lived a woman, an Aborigine, who longed for her lost tribe, and for the stories that had belonged to her people; for she could remember only the happenings of her own Dreamtime. But the old Dreamtime had stolen the stories and hidden them. The woman knew that she must search for the old stories – and through them she might find her tribe again.

Before she set off, she looked for her yam-stick and dilly-bag, but Time had stolen these, too. She found a sugar-bag that the ants had left and which Time had forgotten to destroy, and she picked it up and carried it with her wherever she went. Time laughed at her efforts; he thought her new dilly-bag was useless.

One day, as she searched, the woman came upon the ashes of a fire her own tribe had kindled long ago. Tears came to her eyes, for she yearned for her tribe, and felt lonely. She sat down by the ashes and ran her fingers through the remains of the fire that had once glowed there. And as she looked at the ashes, she called to Biami the Good Spirit to help her find her tribe.

Biami told her to go to the paperbark-trees and ask them to give her some of their bark. The paperbark-trees loved this woman who had lost her tribe, and they gave her their bark. They knew she was not greedy and would not take more than she needed. So she put the bark in her dilly-bag.

Then Biami told the woman to return to the dead fire of her tribe, collect all the charred sticks, and place these, too, in her bag – and to do this each time she came upon the dead fire of any lost tribe.

Time did not understand what the woman was doing, so he followed her.

She travelled far and wide over the earth, and each time she came upon the dead fire of a lost tribe, she would gather the charred sticks, and when at last her bag was filled with them, she went to the secret dreaming-places of the old tribes. Here she rested and again called to Biami, and asked him to help her remember the old stories, so that through them she might find her tribe.

Biami loved this woman, and he put into her mind a new way in which she might find those stories and her tribe. The woman sat down and drew from her bag the charred pieces of stick she had taken from the dead fires, and placed the paperbark flat upon the ground. She drew the sticks across the paperbark, and saw that they made marks on its surface.

So she sat for many years, marking the paperbark with the stories of the long-lost tribes, until she had used up all the charred remnants she had gathered and her bag was empty. In this way she recalled the stories of the old Dreamtime, and through them entered into the old life of the tribes.

And when next the paperbark-trees filled the air with the scent of their sweet, honey-smelling flowers, they took her into their tribe as one of their own, so that she would never again be without the paperbark she needed for her work. They called her Oodgeroo. And this is the story of how Oodgeroo found her way back into the old Dreamtime. Now she is happy, because she can always talk with the tribes whenever she wants to. Time has lost his power over her because Biami has made it so.[5]

Aboriginal Australians organised their own demonstration in Sydney to coincide with the official celebrations there on 26 January 1988. They and their white supporters marched through the streets in a column that stretched for eight kilometres. There was even the active support of a group of doctors, including her old friend Julianne Schwenke, who had since taken up medicine; they volunteered to mix in with the marchers, some of whom were frail or elderly, in order to provide medical attention, if needed.

As Oodgeroo took her place in the eight kilometre long column that day she felt that all the hard work of the last thirty years by both white and Aboriginal Australians had been worthwhile. Support for Aboriginal rights was growing and being seen in city streets. As activist Kevin Gilbert put it: "Two hundred years after the original theft it is still possible for public opinion to make governments cease compounding the felony and make restitution to the victims."[6]

We Are Going
For Grannie Coolwell

They came into the little town
A semi-naked band subdued and silent,
All that remained of their tribe.
They came here to the place of their old bora ground
Where now the many white men hurry about like ants.
Notice of estate agents reads: "Rubbish May Be Tipped Here."
Now it half covers the traces of the old bora ring.
They sit and are confused, they cannot say their thoughts:
"We are as strangers here now, but the white tribe are the strangers.
We belong here, we are of the old ways.
We are the corroboree and the bora ground,
We are the old sacred ceremonies, the laws of the elders.
We are the wonder tales of Dream Time, the tribal legends told.
We are the past, the hunts and the laughing games, the wandering
    camp fires.
We are the lightning-bolt over Gaphembah Hill
Quick and terrible,
And the Thunder after him, that loud fellow.
We are the quiet daybreak paling the dark lagoon.
We are the shadow-ghosts creeping back as the camp fires burn low.
We are nature and the past, all the old ways
Gone now and scattered.
The scrubs are gone, the hunting and the laughter.
The eagle is gone, the emu and the kangaroo are gone from this place.
The bora ring is gone.
The corroboree is gone.
And we are going."

For Oodgeroo the march was a culmination of the Aboriginal civil rights movement. She felt at one with the thousands around her, and knew that they were all enjoying the fruits of FCAATSI's work. She looked back to the time when she had been one of the very few black activists among many white crusaders for Aboriginal rights. She thought of the good work done by white supporters in exposing the continuing plight of the black people; and how good use had been made of the camera, powerful media tool, to expose atrocities, such as the chaining of Aborigines to logs during a dispute over wages in the Northern Territory.

A certain film back in the fifties had had the effect of politicising an important group of white sympathisers in Victoria. It had come about as a result of investigations by West Australian politicians into the aftermath of the British atomic tests at Maralinga that began in the mid fifties. Many groups of Aborigines had been rounded up from the desert, where they had been self-supporting, and placed in disgraceful camps in the Warburton Ranges with no means of fending for themselves. The West Australian Parliament set up a select committee to make an inspection of the area, which they filmed, and Doug (later Sir Douglas) Nicholls, an Aborigine and Lutheran pastor, was asked to join them. The film recorded the horrifying conditions: starving children with swollen bellies; emaciated adults gnawing on bones; flies feeding on the diseased eyes of the many trachoma sufferers – a real-life horror movie. Doug Nicholls brought the film to Victoria where it was shown by the Save the Aborigines Committee in Melbourne; its effect was such that the Committee, whose aims were of a charitable nature, dissolved itself, and the Victorian Aboriginal Advancement League was formed, its charter to obtain full civil rights for Aborigines. Gordon Bryant was the inaugural president and Stan Davies was secretary – once again, membership was largely white. Black Australians had to be awakened to the need to make *their* voices heard.

Some government initiatives had been taken. In 1973 a National Aboriginal Consultative Committee (NACC) was conceived and set up by the Whitlam government. But "it was a powerless body with no secretariat of its own and no funds to call itself together."[7] It was abolished and replaced by the National Aboriginal Conference – an initiative of the Fraser coalition government. Aboriginal activists and their supporters knew that they would never achieve substantial restitution for the land stolen by government initiatives alone. What was needed was a treaty signed by all political parties.

There had been active campaigning for a treaty since 1979. The bicentenary came and went but still there was no treaty. Almost 90 per cent of white Australians voted for the enfranchisement of Aboriginal Australians in the 1967 referendum but in the twenty-one years to the bicentenary neither Labor nor Liberal governments passed any realistic laws to restore Aboriginal rights. The problem arguably lay with governments rather than the constituents.

The push for a treaty was led by a committee of distinguished citizens and sponsored by a long list of well-known Australians – an impressive pressure-group to carry their point, one would have thought. But the Hawke government managed to slide away from a treaty and to substitute a vague promise – "a process of reconciliation". The Aboriginal and Torres Strait Islanders Council (ATSIC) is a product of this watered-down initiative.

In 1988 Australia also hosted the International Exposition, which was held in Brisbane. Unlike the organisers of the bicentennial celebrations, those responsible for the Australia Pavilion at Expo wanted to acknowledge the original occupation of this country by the Aborigines. One idea was to ask a certain Canadian writer to script it, but Andrew Pittendgrich, marketing director of The Production Group, who won the contract, thought differently; he went to Moongalba to talk Oodgeroo into doing something about it. At first her reaction was negative, even hostile. The commercial nature of Expo and its lauding of advanced technologies had no appeal whatever for her; but when she heard that the task was to fall to a Canadian, her arm was twisted! She agreed to a proposal that she write the script for the Rainbow Serpent Theatre under the auspices of The Production Group. The work was commissioned by the Australian Pavilion in association with the Department of Arts, Sport, the Environment, Tourism and the Territories.

Some time later, Anne Derham, production manager for The Production Group, visited Oodgeroo at Moongalba. She was expecting the same treatment Andrew Pittendgrich had received on his first visit.

> I expected to be growled at, lectured, treated with suspicion, ignored, probably abused and possibly told to turn around and go right back to Melbourne.
>
> But it was nothing like that. I was lectured and growled at, but I wasn't ignored. I wasn't treated with suspicion, nor did I have to retrace my steps. I did cop some abuse though; but it was late, we were tired and the port and lemon juice fuelled the fire. I stayed a week, and in that week, the lectures, and growlings opened my eyes in a way that should happen to everyone. I remember that week well, and everything that followed.[8]

She soon developed an affinity for Moongalba.

> It wasn't like anywhere else on North Stradbroke–Minjerribah…But it soon felt like home to me, and in many emotional ways, it still does. It is lush rainforest with a slightly winding, sandy track past trees with shields and snakes carved and brightly painted in the colours of the original Australians. I knew I'd arrived at a place that was private and linked to [Oodgeroo] in a way that I might never understand.

It was unfortunate that Expo coincided with the bicentenary, for many Aborigines living in the southeast area of Queensland confused the two events. They knew they wanted to boycott any celebrations associated with the bicentenary – which included Expo, they thought. Oodgeroo came in for some unwarranted criticism from Aboriginal activists in the Brisbane region. Even Vivian tried to get her to give it up, and Oodgeroo had been hoping to use his help on *The Rainbow Serpent*. Her discussions with him helped to articulate her ideas about her involvement. She explained that this was a once-in-a-lifetime chance to present to people of all nations the time-honoured culture and beliefs of Aboriginal Australians. Vivian was soon convinced and the fruitful collaboration between mother and son began.

Vivian and Kath discuss a stage design for the Yeti Theatre with which they worked in the late sixties.

Artist Son
To Kabul of the tribe Noonuccal (Vivian Walker)

My artist son,
Busy with brush, absorbed in more than play,
Untutored yet, striving alone to find
What colour and form can say,
Yours the deep human need,
The old compulsion, ever since man had mind
And learned to dream,
Adventuring, creative, unconfined.
Even in dim beginning days,
Long before written word was known,
Your fathers too fashioned their art
Who had but bark and wood and the cave stone.
Much you must learn from others, yes,
But copy none; follow no fashions, know
Art the adventurer his lone way
Lonely must go.
Paint joy, not pain,
Paint beauty and happiness for men,
Paint the rare insight glimpses that express
What tongue cannot or pen;
Not for reward, acclaim
That wins honour and opens doors,
Not as ambition toils for fame,
But as the lark sings and the eagle soars.
Make us songs in colour and line:
Painting is speech, painter and poet are one.
Paint what you feel more than the thing you see,
My artist son.

I'm sure that the determination to keep teaching and to touch people with the message of the Rainbow Serpent was why she agreed to work with us. She saw this the way we did, a chance to reach people one more time with the simple message that in our differences we are so much the same.

The assignment was something of a tall order. Oodgeroo and Vivian (who now called himself Kabul Oodgeroo) went to Melbourne to discuss their ideas with The Production Group. Oodgeroo made certain demands, all of which were met: ten actors were to be employed, all of them Aborigines; they were to be paid above Actors' Equity rates for the duration; and they were to be comfortably housed and catered for in quarters close to the Expo site.

Now it was up to Oodgeroo and Kabul to satisfy the demands of the pavilion organisers. They had nine months to put together a script that would last precisely eight and a half minutes. Together they went to work. They wanted the theme to relate to the age-old beliefs in the Earth Mother and that symbol of the giver and taker of life, the Rainbow Serpent.

They both worked hard and long on the script, reading it aloud to each other. "Oh no! Twenty minutes. How do we cut it down? Oh no! Twelve minutes – but what can we take out?" Slowly the work began to take shape. There were drafts and re-drafts, discussions, and government approvals to be sought and obtained before the casting could proceed. But eventually they did it – magic was in the making.

The selection of ten actors for the narrator's role was a demanding task.

> The casting…consisted of trips to all capital cities, after we had issued notices and applications for auditions. The people responded from all over the place – as far north as the Kimberley, as far outback as Quilpie; some came from cities. But they all understood that it would take a lot from them in the way of patience and determination. At the same time, they had doubts and suspicions which, in some cases, never left them.

After many months of intense hard work, millions of dollars, and the commitment and dedication of the production team of Anne Derham, Christine Aspinall and Lindy Marshall, *The Rainbow Serpent* was ready to be seen by an audience of three million. Oodgeroo's supreme contribution was acknowledged in a tribute by Anne Derham:

> Overall, everyone on the project worked as hard as they had ever known. Maybe not physically, but the emotional effort was immense for us all. Through all of it, Oodgeroo was our rock, our mother and our counsel. She was also the disciplinarian, the go-between, the negotiator. Through her, everyone who worked on the project was able to draw the courage and patience to move forward in the face of black criticism, white doubt and everyone's bureaucracy.

In the production remarkable visual effects were time-linked with the script. Performances ran between 10 a.m. and 10 p.m. every day for six months. With some four minutes to clear one audience and admit another, it was a demanding schedule. The actors worked in shifts in the role of The Narrator. A member of The Production Group calculated that there were 10,040 performances.

The essential message of the drama is contained in the lines:

We are different, you and me. We say the earth is our mother – we cannot own her, she own us.

The Narrator says:

Since the Alcheringa, that thing you fulla call Dreamtime, this place has given man shelter from the heat, a place to paint, to dance the sacred dance and talk of his spirit.
How does one repay such gifts?
By protecting the land.

Oodgeroo's ancestral ties to the waters of Moreton Bay (Quandamooka) are soon identified:

Grow strong, Kabul, come back to your children, the mountains, the trees and our father the sky. Come bring us your birds of many colours. Come back to your rivers rushing to Quandamooka. Come back to your teeming fish of a thousand colours and shapes.[9]

The Rainbow Serpent

"The Rainbow Serpent" was written by Oodgeroo and her son Kabul (Vivian Walker). It was first performed at Brisbane Expo in 1988.

Well, gidday, gidday, all you earth fullas. Come, sit down, my country now.

I see you come into sacred place of my tribe to get the strength of the Earth Mother. That Earth Mother…

We are different you and me. We say the earth is our mother – we cannot own her, she own us.

This rock and all these rocks are alive with her spirit. They protect us, all of us…

This land is the home of the Dreamtime. The spirits came and painted themselves on these walls so that man could meet here, grow strong again and take this strength back into the world.

This my totem, Kabul. You know her as the Carpet Snake. She my tribe's symbol of the Rainbow Serpent, the giver and taker of life…

When the spirits of men have been made strong again by Kabul, she'll come back to this earth…

But she send her spirit ones with message sticks to help us take time. To remember. To care for her special things.

First there is Dooruk, the emu, with the dust of the red Earth Mother still on his feet. He come to remind us to protect the land, to always put back as much as we take.

Then there is Kopoo, the big red kangaroo, the very colour of the land. He come to remind us to always take time for ourselves.

And Mungoongarlie, the goanna, last of all because his legs are short. He bring the news that we, his children, are forgetting to give time to each other.

But the animals of the Earth Mother come to say more than this. They come to say that our creator, that Rainbow Serpent, she get weak with anger and grief for what we are doing to this earth.

But here now you fullas. You come sit down by my fire. Warm yourselves and I will tell you the story of how this world began…

Kabul is the mother of us all. She is the spirit of the land – all its beauty, all its colour. But there are those who see no colour, who will not feel the beauty of this land – who wish only to destroy the mother and themselves.

Their eyes are open but they do not see...

Like my ancestors before me, I will always come back to this place to share the feeling of the land with all living things. I belong here where the spirit of the Earth Mother is strong in the land and in me.

Take time you earth fullas. Let the spirit of this mighty land touch you as it touches my people.[10]

Oodgeroo and Vivian were often stopped in the street by conservationists who thanked them heartily for reminding people of the need to care for the Earth Mother. One incident affected Oodgeroo deeply. An American Indian had come to Expo and found his way to a back entrance to the pavilion, pleading to be allowed in. They let him in, and, with tears running down his face, he walked with excitement around the actors, producers and crew, shaking every hand and saying "Thank you, thank you". Clearly, he recognised that his ancestors and Australia's indigenous people shared a tradition of respect for the earth.

In *Wisdom of the Elders*, Peter Knudtson and David Suzuki urge the reader to bear in mind the balance that exists between man and all the other life forms that give him sustenance and shelter. They quote Chief Seattle in a speech delivered in 1854: "All things are connected...whatever befalls the earth befalls the sons of the earth."[11] That, most certainly, is also the message of *The Rainbow Serpent*.

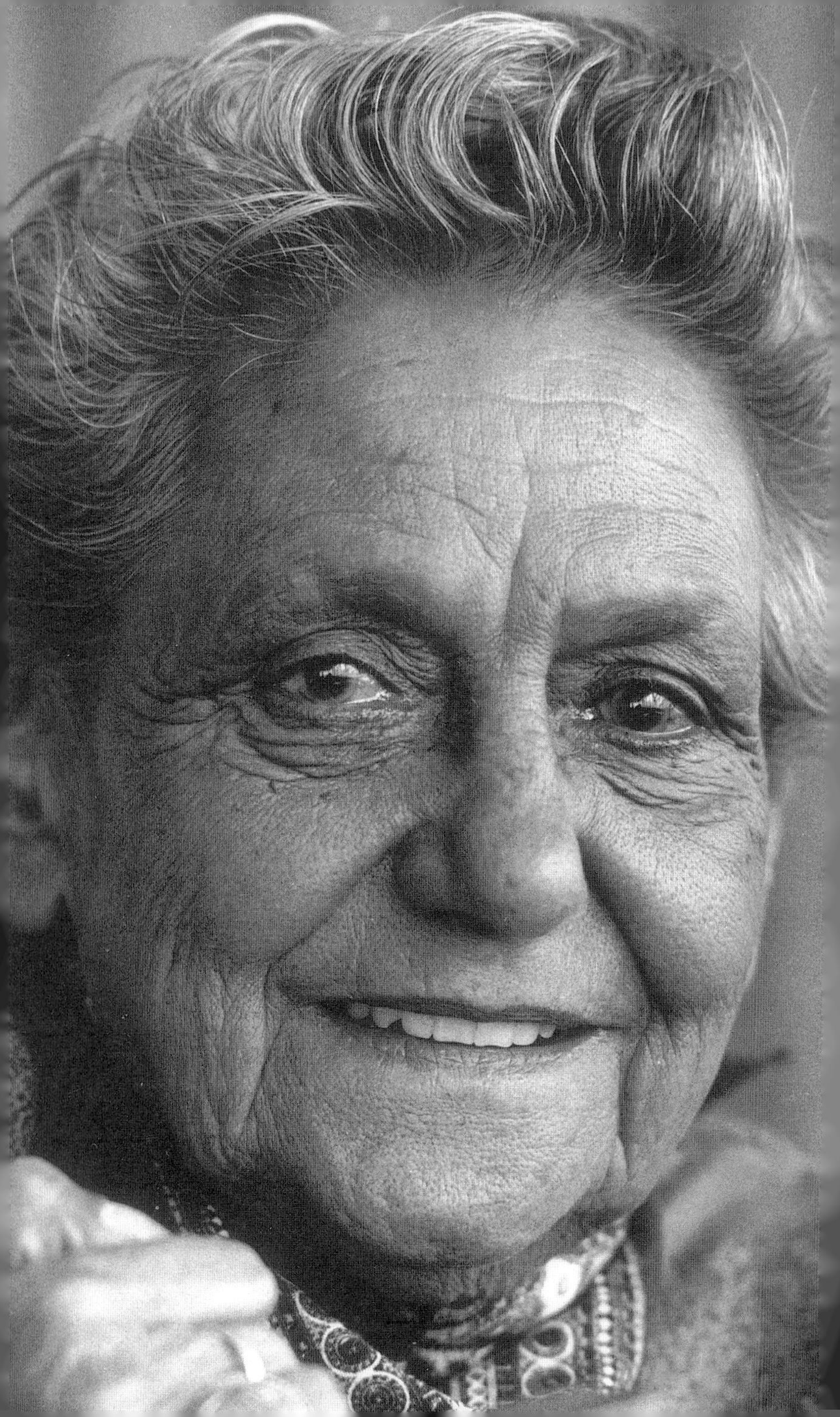

This Little Now

Shortly before Oodgeroo's birthday on 3 November 1990, Bob and I decided to ring and ask if we could pay her a visit on the day. We knew she had never been much inclined to take notice of her birthdays, but I thought she might appreciate some acknowledgment of this special birthday, her seventieth, biblically designated man's natural span.

"Oh well look, Kathie – you'd better not come on Saturday. I'll be manning a polling booth. Come on Sunday or Monday."

What polling booth was this? we wondered. It turned out to be an election in which we, as white Australians, had no right to vote, the first such election in history. The poll was to elect members to regional councils which were to work with the federal government; the new body was to be the Aboriginal and Torres Strait Islanders Council (ATSIC), the Hawke government's initiative. Its intention, in the opinion of Aboriginal activists, was to undermine the demands of the Aboriginal Treaty Committee. Its declared purpose was to hand over to elected Aboriginal groups some responsibility for administering the funds that the Commonwealth set aside for Aboriginal welfare each year. The idea was that they could put forward new models for self-management and have some input into the drafting of legislation affecting Aboriginal people.

As a concession to the rights that were long overdue to the indigenous people, this proposal was seen as lame, tame and altogether inadequate. None the less it was a small step in the right direction, and on a national scale. About sixty regional councils around the country were to liaise with a central committee in Canberra. Unfortunately this body had the final say in all decision-making, and Aboriginal members were in the minority. Appointments were made by the Department of Aboriginal Affairs; nine-tenths of committee appointees were white public servants.

Some Aborigines declared that ATSIC should be boycotted because it did not go far enough, but Oodgeroo and many other activists perceived that it was a half-loaf of participation in decision-making that must be seen as better than the no bread of non-participation that had been their lot for two hundred years.

ATSIC was not destined to make a great impact on the well-being and civil rights of Aborigines; nor has it played a role in that reconciliation between indigenous and white Australians that the federal government likes to talk about. In some cases, the councils have created resentment and hostility among local groups. When Oodgeroo served on the polling booth on her birthday in 1990 her unfailing optimism made her believe that involvement in the work of the councils would be of educational value for those elected. Perhaps, she hoped, the descendants of the elders would be relearning the importance of communal decision-making.

We made our birthday visit, two days after the election, on Monday 5 November. After taking a water-taxi across Moreton Bay – the car ferry had become a monopoly and its charges were prohibitive – we caught a bus to Moongalba and went up to Oodgeroo's rather stylish residence.

When she had first returned to the island in 1971, she had lived in a gunyah for a time until several bouts of bronchitis and medical advice succeeded in persuading her to buy a small caravan. Her life had also been made more comfortable by the arrival of a man who invited himself to live at Moongalba. John O'Brien, a drop-out from the world of white people, had walked away from his own family. He had always found Aboriginal people ready to accept him, and Oodgeroo was no exception. She bought another caravan for herself and gave the first one to John. He fitted in to Moongalba very well and became of great value to her, acting as caretaker when she was away and co-guardian at all times.

Among many friends Oodgeroo made over the years at Moongalba were Ian Gaillard and Keith Gasteen, keen conservationists and Aboriginal rights supporters, who had brought groups of children to visit from northern New South Wales. When these two young men discovered that perfectly good building materials used in the Rainbow Serpent Theatre at Expo were destined for the rubbish dump, they salvaged as much as they could carry away from the site and took the load across to Moongalba. With the materials they built a round open structure for talking sessions, a tin addition to John's caravan to give him extra living space and for Oodgeroo a remarkably pleasant bed-sitting room which was sturdy and roomy. Another young friend, Paul Pailson, converted an old hot water system into a warming stove for the new dwelling.

Ian and Keith also built a verandah, the upright supports being made from rough-finished treetrunks. Oodgeroo honoured her totem, Kabul (*"you know her as the carpet snake"*) with mobiles she made by painting sections of the twisted yerrol vine. As they revolved in the breeze they seemed to come alive. They reminded Oodgeroo of the carpet snake her father had encouraged as a visitor in her childhood home. The children were taught to respect Carpie, but Mrs Ruska had always distrusted it.

Oodgeroo deeply appreciated the fine contribution of these men, given so humbly and with such goodwill. Many honours had been heaped on her over the years, but this kind and practical gift touched her deeply.

Carpet Snake

My father belonged to the Noonuccal tribe of Stradbroke Island, and the carpet snake was his totem. He made sure he looked after his blood brother. My mother belonged to a different tribe. The carpet snake was not her totem. She hated old Carpie, because of his thieving ways. She was proud of her fowl-run and of the eggs our hens provided. Carpie liked the fowl-run too; every time he felt hungry he would sneak in, select the choicest fowl in the run, and swallow it. He could always outsmart Mother, no matter what she did to keep her chooks out of his ravenous belly. But, somehow, Mother never was game enough to bring down the axe on Carpie's head. We all knew she was often tempted to do just that. I think two things stopped her:

her deep respect for the fact that Dad's decisions were final around the house, and the thought that if she killed in anger, Biami the Good Spirit would punish her.

We all loved Carpie except for Mother – and the dog. The dog kept well out of Carpie's way, because he was scared stiff of him. He seemed to know that a ten-foot carpet snake can wind itself around a dog and in time swallow it whole.

Whenever Mother thought none of us kids was around, she would swear at old Carpie – and Mother's swearing could outmatch that of any bullocky anywhere in Australia.

…I used to like it when I went off to the lavatory and found him holed up there. He would stretch himself right out across a beam in the ceiling. I used to sit in the lavatory for hours and tell him my innermost secrets, and it was very satisfying the way old Carpie would never interrupt the conversation or crawl away. Mother often accused me of dodging chores by going off and spending such a long time in the lavatory. This wasn't quite true; all I wanted to do was to share my secrets with Carpie.

When Dad died, we lost Carpie. He just seemed to disappear. We never found out what happened to him. Perhaps Biami the Good Spirit whispered to him: "Your blood brother has gone to the shadow land. Your days are numbered. Get lost."[1]

We had brought with us a picnic lunch for five, expecting also to see John and Vivian. John came down from his caravan (with a dear little Australian Terrier puppy), and Oodgeroo told us she had been pleased to receive a birthday phonecall from her old friend Merle Thornton in Melbourne.

"Where's Vivian?" I asked.

"He's gone away – he wouldn't stay to see you. He doesn't want people to see him, he's so emaciated. He looks terrible and he couldn't bear you to see him."

Now we felt sure about what we'd feared ever since Oodgeroo had told us that Vivian had been in hospital in Sydney suffering from an unusual and very severe form of bronchitis: we had heard that a special kind of pneumonia was often a first sign of AIDS. But since then we had seen Vivian – at the Malcolm Williamson concert about a year ago and more recently, in April, at the launch of *Kath Walker in China* – and on both occasions he had looked his usual self. But our fears were well founded.

He didn't want us to know: dear, friendly, kind and cheerful Vivian, friend of my kids and loved by all who had looked after him when Oodgeroo had been active in the civil rights movement.

"You can't hide it forever, it's like pregnancy, it will show," Oodgeroo had said to him. "But", she told us, "it was his decision."

After lunch Oodgeroo took us in her elderly Holden to see some of the facilities she had been responsible for establishing. Although the Moongalba of her dreams had not become a reality, she *had* been able to bring together the Aboriginal people in the area and help them to form a co-operative. The North Stradbroke Island Aboriginal and Islander Housing Co-operative Society Limited was incorporated as a Community Advancement Society on 8 September 1980. A community-oriented project, it offered a wide range of services to the general community as well as to the Aboriginal and Islander residents. Its main

Original premises of the
Aboriginal Housing and
Health Centre, Dunwich

THIS LITTLE NOW • 147

role was to provide housing for disadvantaged families, and the first to benefit were three needy families at One Mile who moved into brand new houses in Dunwich.

In the ten years of its existence the Housing Co-operative had acquired its own building, which Oodgeroo took us to visit. We met many of the people whose dedication had enabled it to extend its services greatly. In 1984 a medical service was started. The doctor on duty when we were there was Wendy Page; her medical advice was available three days a week to any person of any race who chose to consult her. Since 1985, a fund assisted people to meet funeral expenses; it was wholly dependent upon community donations and fund-raising activities. Since January 1986, social welfare assistance has been available to families or individuals in crisis; funding came from the Queensland Council of Social Service (QCOSS), the state professional association of social workers. Then, in May 1988, a playgroup for children under six was established, offering parents and children four sessions a week. Known as the Kin Kin Playgroup, it was approved and subsequently funded by the federal Department of Health, Housing and Community Services. A year later, a scheme for vacation care programmes started up, approved and funded by the same department.

When we arrived at the latest of the Co-operative's initiatives, we stepped out of the car in front of what looked like a giant galvanised-iron shed.

"See that," said Oodgeroo, with such pride that I felt we ought to be looking at Buckingham Palace. The notice-board proclaimed that we were looking at a Learning Centre attached to the Redland Community College. Inside, one room was equipped for clerical training (complete with brand new computers), and another for trade training, with workbenches and tools. The centre was very new and like a huge barn, with plenty of room for expansion.

In order to get the Learning Centre started, a group of unemployed local Aboriginal youth were declared to be foundation students; they were involved in every part of the construction "from clearing the land to driving home the last nail".[2]

Not quite two years later I asked Oodgeroo if we could visit the Co-operative again to see how all the services were progressing. She agreed, promising to prepare the people working at the centre to talk to us, but said she would keep away herself in case her presence inhibited anyone from speaking openly. But we heard only words of praise. Not only had all the original initiatives flourished, but new ones had been added, and the established ones extended. Earlier that year thirty students had graduated from college courses at the Learning Centre in diverse fields that included computer accounting; word processing; garment production; small business management; wood sculpture; and nursery and landscape practices. The Learning Centre was now financed by both ATSIC and the (federal) Department of Employment, Education and Training. Although most programmes were designed to train young Aborigines for entry into the white-dominated workforce, Aboriginal culture was not forgotten. The Aboriginal Culture Studies course covered "a wide range of issues from traditional 'way of life' to contemporary society and the problems that cause conflict within a community because of the lack of understanding".[3] The centre also set up its own NAIDOC Week Celebrations Committee to contribute to the National Aborigines and Islanders Day Observance Committee.

The Minjerribah Nursery, another initiative of the Co-operative, provides employment for local students who have completed the nursery and landscaping course at the Learning Centre. The six hectares just north of Dunwich on which the Learning Centre building is situated is an ideal location for the nursery.

With the help of the Department of Social Security (DSS) a community agency was set up in November 1991 to serve the residents of North Stradbroke in relation to DSS enquiries. The latest initiative is a National Parks and Wildlife Services agency which provides training, skills and employment on the island and promotes awareness of Aboriginal traditions.

Mary Martin, a nurse on call twenty-four hours a day, provided most of the information we wanted during our visit. When I asked her how much these developments owed to Oodgeroo, she replied "Pretty well all

of them – she has the nous, the courage and the skills to make it happen."
Dr Wendy Page later reinforced this: she believed that what Oodgeroo had achieved, at considerable cost to herself, was little short of a miracle.

The Co-operative was working well, thanks to the enthusiasm of all involved; workers shared a sense of purpose and had developed a greater awareness of their cultural identity and their local history. Projects for the future were detailed in an impressive document, *Strategic Development Plans, 1991–2001*.

Vivian died on 20 February 1991, aged thirty-eight. When he felt certain that his death was close he went off to Sydney to make things easier for Oodgeroo. Vivian told her she would be pilloried when his condition became public, but she had always said to him, "I'm happy to tell the world you've got AIDS and I still love you." Later, she told me that when she had visited Vivian in Sydney's Prince Henry Hospital when he had the AIDS-related bronchitis, she was shocked to discover that some similarly afflicted patients had been completely rejected by their families.

She was determined to carry out Vivian's wish to be buried at Moongalba. Denis had been a tower of strength to Oodgeroo in the last weeks of Vivian's illness, and he now played a key role in the funeral arrangements. Accompanied by an Anglican minister friend, he met the plane at the Brisbane airport and transported the coffin back to the island in a van.

A deep grave was dug for Mother Earth to receive back her son. At the ceremony many of Vivian's young friends from the theatre, both Aboriginal and white, were invited to speak extemporaneously. And so Vivian was laid to rest among the trees and shrubs and wildflowers of the land – the domain of his Noonuccal ancestors for countless centuries. From time to time, his friends come to visit the grave; usually they bring a young tree to plant so that as old trees die, new ones will replace them.

Vivian and Oodgeroo

John Collins has commented that in Vivian's "last few years [he] had become his mother's closest critic and confidant". With his death

> her faith was tested as never before. In public she had always remained strong, resilient and ready at all times to be provocative, with a piercing wit and a menacing intellect. But the loss of a son who was taking on his mother's weapon of language and adding to it with his very substantial artistic talent was almost too much to bear.[4]

Now herself in the last few years of life, Oodgeroo continued to work tirelessly, attending ATSIC meetings as an elected member of the southeast region and investigating possibilities of getting land grants to Aboriginal groups who could establish a claim through past "ownership". In the Aboriginal context, land was not owned – it was occupied and

The poem "Son of Mine" is displayed on a plaque in Oodgeroo's honour on the concourse of the Sydney Opera House.

cared for as a supporter of life for the plants, animals and people. As Judith Wright has written:

> For Aborigines, every part of the country they occupied, every mark and feature was numinous with meaning. The spirit ancestors had made the country itself, in their travels, and fused each part of it into the "Dreamtime" – a continuum of past, present and future – that was also the unchangeable law by which Aborigines lived.[5]

Oodgeroo was well aware that the past can never be brought back, but she, like many other Aborigines, would dearly have loved to restore to Aboriginal care some portions of the ancient continent. Her determined efforts to make Moongalba a centre where all people could be acquainted with Aboriginal lore, customs and the spiritual ties that perpetuate Aborigines' respect for Mother Earth surely should have received more official recognition than they have to date.

Since Moongalba was established, over thirty thousand children have experienced its uniqueness. Children were always the centre of Oodgeroo's concern, holding the key to a brighter future in which racial differences would be welcomed as enriching for society. When opportunities to speak to children arose, she never spared herself. School visits were a continuing activity during the eighties and, as late as July 1992, in Toowoomba, she visited twenty-three schools in five days. Attitudes *were* changing, she believed: in today's schoolrooms, Australian, Chinese, Indian and Vietnamese classmates are likely to be more sensitive to the rights of Aboriginal people than their parents were.

In 1991 Oodgeroo was asked to be fellow-in-residence during second semester at the St George campus of the University of New South Wales. Dr Rhonda Craven, a lecturer in Social Studies, was co-ordinator of a project on which she and Oodgeroo would work to develop curricula in Aboriginal Studies for trainee teachers. Together they designed teachers' handbooks. Oodgeroo made it clear that white and Aboriginal children should be taught Aboriginal Studies in the same classroom. She spoke to Professor Tony Vincent about the importance of instructing teachers in how to teach the subject; he wrote to the federal minister, Robert Tickner, and obtained a grant to facilitate the project.

In 1994 there were seven universities in Australia whose Education departments were trialling the course she and Rhonda designed, and it was Oodgeroo's hope that Aboriginal Studies would become a mandatory subject in all primary schools. The entire project is dedicated to her.

As part of the Brisbane Biennial in May 1993, the Queensland Theatre Company premiered *One Woman's Song*, a play about the early life of

Oodgeroo by Peta Murray. She dedicated the play to "Oodgeroo of the Tribe Noonuccal and to the older, wiser women, of all tribes, who have so much to teach us, if only we will listen."

With the role of Oodgeroo at different ages shared by Lydia Miller, Deborah Mailman and Neokigai Bonner and with music by Yothu Yindi's Michael Havir, the production attracted critical acclaim and enjoyed an extended season. Oodgeroo was happy about the play; she had attended rehearsals and gladly contributed her advice.

Her long struggle for the rights of Aborigines, with many disappointments along the way, did not diminish her faith in the future. She related to me a small but significant ceremony that has been adopted by the South-East Queensland Regional Council of ATSIC to close their meetings. Glasses of water are placed on the table – a reminder that alcohol was unknown here before 1788. The toast, from her poem "A Song of Hope", begins:

> *To our fathers' fathers*
> *The pain, the sorrow;*
> [Glasses stay on the table]
>
> *To our children's children*
> *The glad tomorrow.*
> [The glasses are raised and the toast is drunk]

And hope remains.

OPPOSITE:
Oodgeroo wears a shirt made for her by Pat Jarvis, a member of the Dharagh nation of New South Wales; the photo was taken in 1993 on Oodgeroo's last visit to the author's home.

Oodgeroo of the Noonuccal people died in Brisbane on Thursday, 16 September 1993. It was 6.30 in the morning. Denis was at her bedside in the Greenslopes Repatriation Hospital, as was Patty, Denis's ex-wife, Oodgeroo's loving, caring friend.

Her illness was quite short, her time in hospital weeks not months. Her multiple cancers had been explained to her, she knew she was soon to die and she was unafraid. Her friends and relatives who visited her daily were consoled that her suffering was not great; the care of the doctors and nurses could not have been better. The kindness and respect of all comforted her, as did the great bunches of flowers from friends and admirers that filled the room.

Her wish to be buried at Moongalba alongside Vivian was fulfilled. Denis made the arrangements, and the ceremony was conducted before a crowd of hundreds. Many people came forward to speak in her memory. As the mourners filed past the grave, a group of dancers, some of them her grandsons, performed ritual dances.

ABOVE: Kath was buried beside Vivian at Moongalba on 20 September 1993.

RIGHT: Denis Walker, 1993

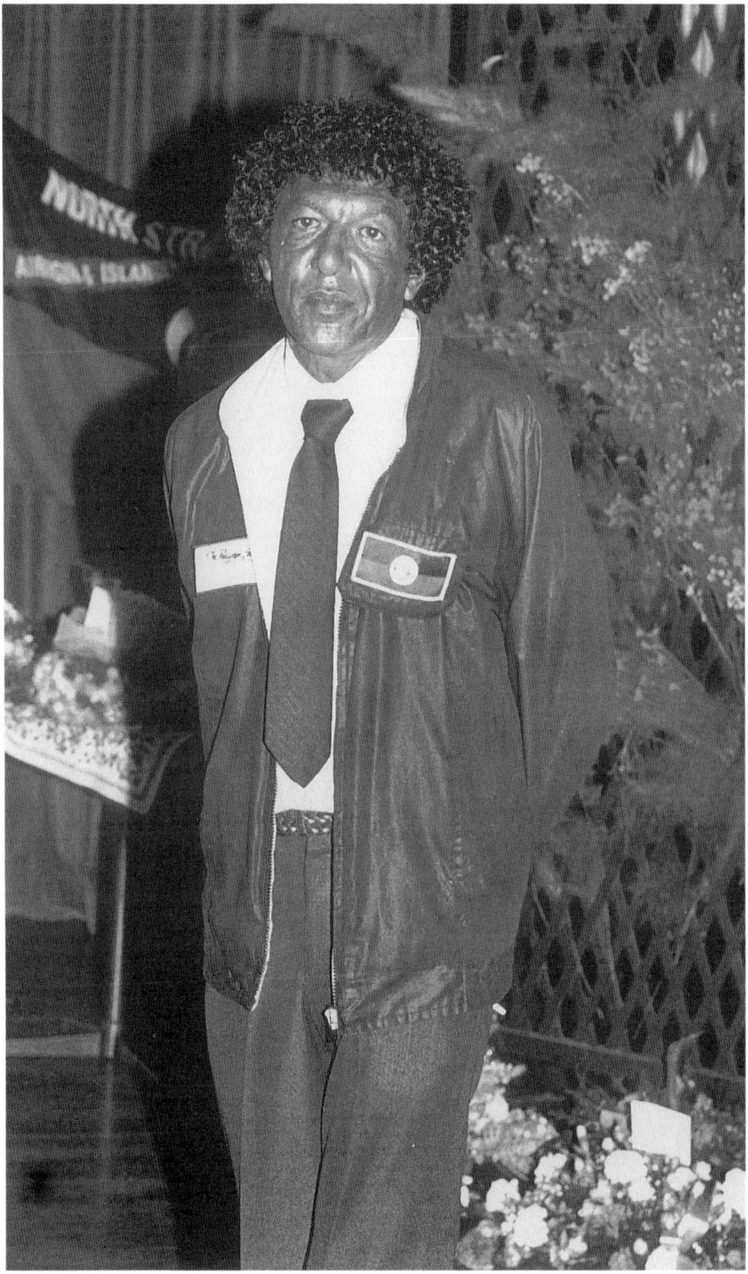

It was a magnificent life, for it did much to build bridges between her people and the children of the white invaders. Her poetry, her belief in the ability of children to live together in harmony, her hopes for a just and peaceful world, all these will survive the great sadness of her death.

In a closing speech to the 1993 conference of the Australian and New Zealand Association for the Advancement of Science Mr Justice Michael Kirby read her poem, "The Past". She would have been pleased.

Ceremonial dances were performed at the graveside.

The Past

Let no one say the past is dead.
The past is all about us and within.
Haunted by tribal memories, I know
This little now, this accidental present
Is not the all of me, whose long making
Is so much of the past.

Tonight here in suburbia as I sit
In easy chair before electric heater,
Warmed by the red glow, I fall into dream:
I am away
At the camp fire in the bush, among
My own people, sitting on the ground,
No walls about me,
The stars over me,
The tall surrounding trees that stir in the wind
Making their own music,
Soft cries of the night coming to us, there
Where we are one with all old Nature's lives
Known and unknown,
In scenes where we belong but have now forsaken.
Deep chair and electric radiator
Are but since yesterday,
But a thousand camp fires in the forest
Are in my blood.
Let none tell me the past is wholly gone.
Now is so small a part of time, so small a part
Of all the race years that have moulded me.

Part Two Poetry

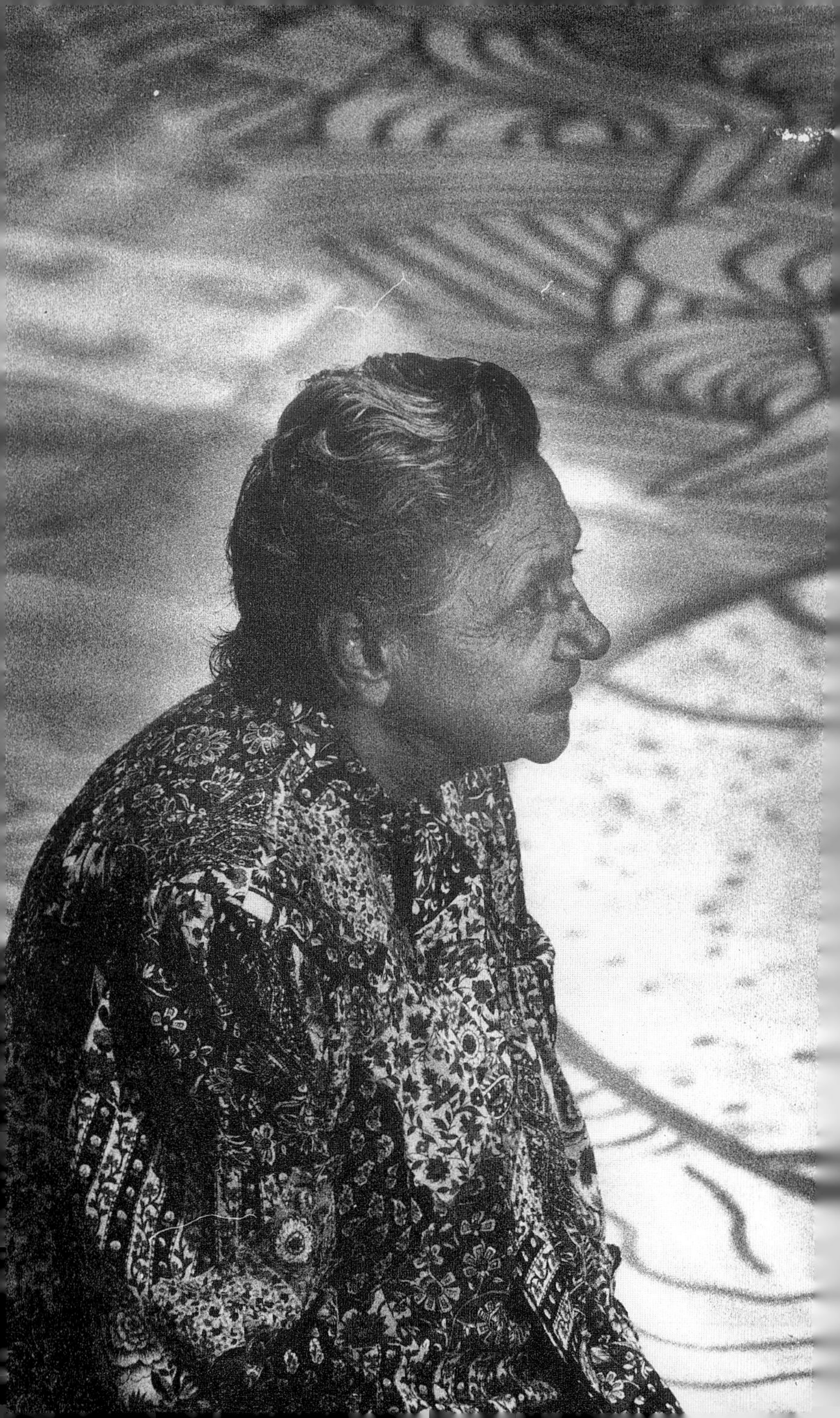

The Poetry
An Appreciation by Judith Wright

Early in the 1960s, I was a part-time reader of poetry manuscripts for Jacaranda Press, the Brisbane publishing firm headed by a young publisher, Brian Clouston. In 1963, a manuscript came to Jacaranda, its author then not known to me. But the poems rang out and commanded attention.

Very little was expected of Queensland, at that time, in the matter of poetry. *Meanjin Papers*, renamed *Meanjin*, had left Brisbane in 1945 for more influential fields in Melbourne; the young Barjai Group, which had published work by a new post-war generation of writers, had vanished, its members mostly now in those southern cities. The Angus & Robertson anthologies of poetry showed few Queensland names. The chief sign of any poetic revival was that of the Realist Writers, strong in Queensland because of John Manifold and Rodney Hall; but then mainly interested in collecting and reviving bush ballads. Kath Walker, I found, was a member of that group, but her work was in a very different field.

She was already known as a fiery young speaker in Aboriginal matters ("agitator" was the word used, in an attempt to link her to the Communist Party, so feared and detested in Queensland. The Realist Writers certainly had Communist members.) But Kath Walker was different. Her poems stood out from the rest, not only because they were voiced by an Aboriginal woman, but because they showed a remarkable quality of courage and a command of language to express their demands.

It happened that, at that time, two conflicting strains had emerged in poetry and literature in Australia. The older, formal and usually conventional, rhymed and metrical verse inherited from an earlier British tradition and enshrined in most English syllabus-settings up to University level – a tradition which since the beginning of the century British writers themselves had begun rejecting – was showing signs of breakdown. New influences were emerging, especially since the war, which had

Oodgeroo visited Judith Wright at her home in Braidwood, New South Wales, in 1993.

brought a new knowledge of American poetry, and had startled white Australians into recognising that the British inheritance, politically and socially, was waning fast. Where Australian Aborigines had never been granted any kind of equal treatment, American Negroes were to be seen in handsome uniforms in city streets, with apparently high pay and good chances in life. Asia seemed to have moved several steps closer to Australia; the implications for the future of the White Australia policy were more alarming than Australians liked to consider. We had been forced to think about what Australia was, and what it might be, and the colonial view of such things no longer seemed immutable. Not Britain, but the USA, was now our protector and hope.

All this disturbing change was accentuated by the fact that, though it was hushed up as much as possible, Australian Aborigines and Torres Strait Islanders were playing a considerable part in the defence of the north during the war. In the Army, they were being treated on much the same basis as whites, fed and housed decently, and trusted as members of the Forces. Kath Walker herself had been a member of the women's forces, I learned, and was a trained telephone operator, and the meagre primary education Aborigines were given had been reinforced by what she learned.

I knew of her as an acknowledged leader in the new Aboriginal movement, which was standing against the harsh "protectionism" which ruled Aborigines in Queensland even more strictly than elsewhere. Moreover, the whole international scene in former European colonies was wilting as the United Nations' Declaration of Human Rights began to take effect. It was the background for Kath's own activism, and formed the basis of the first poem in her manuscript, "Aboriginal Charter of Rights".

I knew Jim Devaney, her adviser in the poems, fairly well; he was an occasional contributor to the first few issues of *Meanjin Papers* and I liked his poems; but they were certainly conventional verse compared to the voice I heard through this manuscript. The poem had been written as a contribution to the proceedings of the fifth annual general meeting of the Federal Council for the Advancement of Aborigines and Torres Strait Islanders in Adelaide that year; it was a galvanising set of demands:

We want hope, not racialism,
Brotherhood, not ostracism,
Black advance, not white ascendance:
Make us equals, not dependents

blazed this new voice in the fields of Aboriginal subjection.

You dishearten, not defend us,
Circumscribe, who should befriend us.
Give us welcome, not aversion,
Give us choice, not cold coercion,
Status, not discrimination,
Human rights, not segregation…

Though baptized and blessed and Bibled
We are still tabooed and libelled.
You devout Salvation-sellers,
Make us neighbours, not fringe-dwellers…

Must we native Old Australians
In our own land rank as aliens?

Those demands, and many more, rang out against a background of long-accepted silence, and they seemed to me imperative. This poetry had to be published and listened to, for it was a challenge and a warning as well as a new achievement.

Was it poetry? It could be set against the general run of largely boring and cliché-ridden verse that thudded on to publishers' desks every day and was promptly sent back; in Queensland in those days there was a lot of it, as I had cause to know, not only as a reader for Jacaranda but in past days for *Meanjin* too. Ideas were few; fire and urgency were nearly non-existent. This stuff was alive.

It isn't easy now to remember the days when Aborigines were silent, nearly invisible, certainly unchallenging. The largely charity-minded whites, the bureaucrat protectors, who made up the few organisations which concerned themselves with "the Aboriginal problem" were to jump as though an electric shock had struck them when the poems were published. They seemed bizarrely dangerous to all preconceptions of what Aborigines were, and all principles of what they should be.

The "protection" method of dealing with the indigenous people had long been the only acceptable response to the "problem". It involved herding Aborigines into white-controlled, white-owned government reserves (which did nothing to protect them from predation by the "protectors" themselves); beyond the reserves were a very few and isolated camping places and town reserves or enclaves in the poorest city suburbs. Since the war, the change in thinking had begun, but it was strongly resisted and very limited. There was a new catch-cry: "assimilation". Those who advocated it, including the very influential Professor A.P. Elkin, for many years head of the only anthropology department in any Australian university, had in mind a strict definition of Aboriginality, which to a large extent followed the official line of demarcation between "pure-blood" and "half-caste".[1] To the uneasy colonial mind, the "pure-blood" was by definition a "savage" – dangerous and in need of education, Christianising and indoctrinating – the "half-caste" was neither Aboriginal nor European, an embarrassment acceptable to nobody. In contrast to the "tribal" Aborigines, who had at least the virtue of being a "pure culture" and worth study on that account, the "part-Aborigines" were seen as without a culture, with no place in academic studies, or for that matter in society itself. They were not truly "native peoples", but a moral liability.

(I remember a trained anthropologist of my acquaintance, deprived of research funding by circumstances, lamenting that the only work she was qualified to do was with Aboriginal peoples, and she could no longer get back to the far north of Australia to continue the work she had started. I pointed out that there were very many Aboriginal people within a radius of only a few miles from where she lived, whose lives would repay a good deal of attention. But for her they had no interest in anthropological study – no research funding was available to work in "half-caste" communities.)

Yet for years past, those communities had begun recovering from their shock and distress, asserting their existence, resenting their status and demanding to be treated as human beings, not as "fringe" outcasts.

They were to be a seed-bed for a new kind of Aboriginality. Here from among them was a voice that couldn't be silenced or intimidated but made claims and voiced accusations that the uneasy hearers knew to be true, however long the facts had been pushed into the background of their minds.

As I read, the razor-edge of the poems was unavoidable. Poems like "White Man, Dark Man" struck home to my own background of confident Anglican superiority:

> *White fellow, true*
> *You had more for pride:*
> *You had Jesus Christ,*
> *But him you crucified,*
> *And still do.*

My own response to the poems, their merciless accusations, their notes of mourning and challenge, was immediate. But I could almost hear the voices of the critics in advance, denying that this was poetry at all, sweeping the accusations and the reproaches under the carpet with a critical broom and dismissing the poems as doggerel. It would be easy to bypass their challenge, in days when Aborigines were regarded as nothings.

If there was one forbidden territory in poetry, in those times when new universities and Arts courses were springing up all over Australia, it was "propaganda and protest" literature, especially in verse. The new academicism that was creeping into Australian poetry, along with the inrush of English graduates and lecturers from abroad, was sharply restrictive. Australian writing was regarded at best as apprentice work, colonial and minor; but the lingering revulsion from the coarse "bush-balladry" and the unsophisticated verse of writers like Lawson involved an instant no-no in critical circles to "mere verse" – let alone verse with political overtones. Poetry could have no social or political intention; "pure poetry" was the only legitimate kind. This was not only so in the derivative literatures of the new Dominions.

In 1963 a contemporary English critic, James Press, published a survey of the poetry of the fifties and early sixties.[2] He identified a "background of change and confusion" in British poetry since the Second World War: "a grating tone of arid self-righteousness", a "tight-lipped narrowness of response" was perceptible, he thought, in the period. "The most striking of these features", he wrote, "is the general retreat from direct comment on or involvement with any social doctrine." This Cold War revulsion from political or social comment was certainly visible in Australian criticism and academic circles in Australia at the time when Kath began to publish.

With few locally educated graduates to fill the new posts, and with a long-standing conservative literary establishment already in place, only a minor revival of bush-balladry opposed that strain in the fifties and sixties (and it was scarcely academically respectable even at its most voguish). To question the acceptance of the reigning inheritance of Romantic, Victorian and Georgian English poetry as models was not a healthy proposition for the careers of young lecturers. Moreover, they had their own internal quarrels and struggles for position to keep them busy as critical schools rose and declined. That "tight-lipped narrowness of response" was not going to be shifted by a young Aboriginal woman's "protest verse".

Pressure was starting for Australian literature to be admitted as a respectable subject for study. A chair in Australian Literature was mooted. But it was not going to be a revolutionary change. Criticism must become professional; unqualified amateurs and mere reviewers would have to be revalued on properly theoretical lines. A canon must be established, and it was not likely that it would find room for Kath Walker.

I looked at my own evaluation of the poems. To me, poetry had little value if it didn't work in sparking response; this manuscript was working, as far as I was concerned. It was "felt along the blood". I told Brian Clouston that the book should be published, not as a curiosity, but as a contribution to Australian poetry in its own right.

Of course, it didn't work out quite like that. The boom in sales which took *We Are Going* through edition after edition did happen partly

Whynot Street

*Officiously they hawked about
"Petition" to keep abos out,
And slavishly, without a peep,
The feeble yes-men signed like sheep.*

*And are we still the ousted, then,
And dare you speak for decent men?
This site was ours, you may recall,
Ages before you came at all.*

*"No abos here!" Why not, Whynot?
And if black-balling and boycott,
First black-ball pride and arrogance,
Boycott this vile intolerance.*

because of its "curiosity value", its first-footing for Aboriginal published work. But its publisher must have been surprised by that response: skyrocketing sales, reception by the public, and instant recognition by readers and purchasers, if not by the academic establishment.

It happened that 1964 was a sharply controversial year, as the black protest movement thrust its way into the limelight. In Brisbane, a group of Aboriginal families had been summarily evicted from their bark and iron shelters at Acacia Ridge to make way for "housing development". That eviction, which would have been taken for granted by the white population a few years before, now provoked an outburst of angry response by Aborigines, and public controversy in the press. A kind of shame was beginning to overtake whites in the face of this protest. Colonialism was coming under historical and international question: the African colonies were emerging from European administration; closer to home, the question of New Guinea was controversial; and the situation of the Pacific Islands under European administration was being raised.

In the Brisbane suburb of West End, residents refused to allow a long-overdue Aboriginal hostel to be built in their street; its name, Whynot Street, was a wide open invitation to Kath's verbal weaponry. Long-suppressed and little publicised rumours of exploitation of Aboriginal pensioners by police, who were the appointed "Protectors" in most country towns, kept rising to the surface. *We Are Going* perhaps sold all the better for the topical application of many of the poems.

But they were not revelations; they mostly corroborated what people knew or suspected. Their import came from the fact of their existence itself. They were startling because they came from a region of Aboriginality that had not been supposed to exist, the city suburbs where few or no so-called "full-blood" Aborigines survived, and where "assimilation" was now the catch-cry, certainly not "survival of Aboriginality". They spoke out the hidden demands of the "fringe-people" for their own values, their own kind of recognition; and they raided reality, not sentimental "salvationism", to do so. The poems refused to be patronised. They demanded rather than pleaded; they spoke not only of oppression, injustice and hardship but of pride, and the right to pride, and the sorrow and loss of Aboriginal life. Above all, they rang of truth.

The title poem, "We Are Going", took on the voice of the old people, the survivors who were nearing the end of their time, and of their sadness in this terrible new world: "We are the past, the hunts and the laughing games, the wandering campfires." But the poem affirmed their rights as well as their loss:

> *We are as strangers here now, but the white tribe are the strangers.*
> *We belong here, we are of the old ways.*
> *We are the corroboree and the bora ground,*
> *We are the old sacred ceremonies, the laws of the elders.*

At a time when the very old and revered, like the elder Willie McKenzie, were almost all that remained of their lost lands, the poem meant a great deal to Aborigines of the southeastern Queensland tribes. Its sad tones echoed for the young newly political rebels like an affirmation of their rights by descent and birth. For sensitive white people, the mournful voices receded as a reproach, and a relief; for the young Aborigines they were a heart-breaking memory.

> *The bora ring is gone.*
> *The corroboree is gone.*
> *And we are going.*

Anyone who couldn't recognise that as a poem, I thought, had very little instinct for poetry. For me, who had seen the deserted bora ring near my grandmother's home, and who knew from my father the fate of New England Aborigines driven by white men with whips and guns over cliffsides for "trespass" or cattle-spearing, but had never known the "pure cultures" anthropologists were now beginning to study, the poem was more moving than any elegy in an English country churchyard.

Judged by the standards applied in English Honours courses, not all the poems in *We Are Going* were as recognisably "poetry" as that. "Tree Grave", "Dawn Wail" – these and a couple of others stood out, on any standards; the political poems worked as they were intended to do, and their sharply pointed comment could hurt and startle readers who had never encountered such criticism before (they were many at that time). Such readers reacted with bitter resentment, sometimes translating that resentment into critical dismissal. But if the protest poems were dismissed, the sting remained. They had a clarity, an incisive quality, that clung to the mind like bindii burrs. That is to say, they were functional, as poetry should be.

Sure enough, the reviewers and critics moved in on them, especially the academically qualified critics. Kath was said to be "not a poet at all"; she had neither the polish of English poetry nor the "authentic voice of the song-man" (the gender distinction was clear). But the public went on buying the book. It had passed its seventh edition when her second book appeared.

As to the authentic voice of the songman, it was more than doubtful whether that voice had been heard at all by literary critics at the time. It had certainly not been hailed or welcomed in the very few translations then available. It was to be many years before such translations were acknowledged as literary influences on Australian poetry.

As the critical hullabaloo went on, Kath, dignified as ever, brought out the second book, *The Dawn Is At Hand*. Published in 1966, it again came at a critical time for the Aboriginal cause. It was to be a kind of manifesto, or text, for the lead-up to the referendum in the following year.

Kath's own foreword to the book made no claims against the judgments of the critical ascendancy. She wrote:

I am well aware that the success of *We Are Going*...was not due to any greatness in my simple verse, but to the fact that it was the work of an Aboriginal. It had therefore what I believe the French call a *succès de curiosité*. Another factor was the sudden and heartening new awareness among whites about that time of the plight of the Aborigines, and the growing demand that something be done about it, which I am proud to think I helped to stimulate...

The chief criticism seemed to be that some of the poems were somewhat angry and bitter; as though even atrocities were never to be mentioned by nice people.

She did, for all that, concede, on Devaney's suggestion, to the view that "propaganda-like stuff" is "not necessarily good in poetry". She was not deferring to the judgments of white critics, nor was she claiming to rival the poetry that they admired, but she firmly stood by her protest poetry as legitimate. This is, of course, the crux of the quarrel the critics had with it. Was it merely because the poems hit home and were painful to the reader that they were judged to be "not poetry at all"? (If so, what becomes of the verse of Swift and Pope?) Or is it really unacceptable that people who are not part of the "system" and have been abused and put down by it should speak against it in the only way that has been made available to them? Should Kath have waited to publish until she had an Honours degree in English Literature? But if she had, as she well might have done, the whole point and function of her verse would have been blunted by that fact alone. It's not a question anyone has wanted to answer.

Her membership of the Realist Writers group, let alone her outspoken opposition to authority, had made her vulnerable to the accusation that her work was "Communist" (a catch-all accusation then for all who disagreed with authority in Queensland and elsewhere). As she wrote in her preface, it was "automatically the answer to every vigorous protest against social injustice". Nor was she, as others accused, inventing the "old tribal tales" which she interpreted in her poems, for "these were heard from the old people when I was a child".

Because so much of what should have been her inheritance of legend and story had been destroyed, she was later to write, in the prose stories published as *Stradbroke Dreamtime*, the tale of her own childhood and her family, and some stories that might have been part of the lost legends. For this too the critics scolded: these were not the authentic tales and therefore weren't legitimate as subjects. In fact, there was little she could do that was accepted as her proper field. Such criticism falls to the ground when its motives are questioned.

In *The Dawn Is At Hand*, she shows a stronger command of imagery and metaphor, as in "Municipal Gum" and "The Past", and continues to use the half-forgotten echoes of the tribal tales. But, as always, the real sting of her work lies in its protests on behalf of her people.

> *Dark unmarried mothers,*
> *Fair game for lechers –*
> *Bosses and station-hands,*
> *And in town and city*
> *Low-grade animals*
> *Prowl for safe prey*

Her anger over the distinction between the rape of white girls and black; her bitter accusation over the "stern talk of maintenance" for the white victims which never applied when the victim was black, should have stung the legal establishment as well as the "salvation-sellers". But "for dark unmarried mothers/the law does not run".

Such distinctions persist and have not changed; but for all that, the way in which Aborigines and their oppression was viewed did take a further step when Kath's voice was raised. If before that there had been no white response to the shames of the dominant culture, it was not quite so easy to shrug away the question now that there was a fearless, and respected, voice to ask it.

So, poetry or not, the books were doing their work. Kath was not just a new phenomenon in Australian literature, she was what she had wanted to be, the voice of a people who had been almost voiceless. The American publication of *We Are Going*, too, was a direct blow in the face of critics who would have been pleased if their own work had been published overseas.

Many poems in this second collection have taken their place in anthologies both in Australia and overseas, as those in the first book had done. Australian anthologists, always conventional and timid in admitting new poets to their collections, at first tended to push the poems to one side. A poem from *We Are Going* appeared in the Angus & Robertson anthology of 1964; but the later anthologies are chary of including them.

A year or two after the publication of *The Dawn Is At Hand*, I undertook an Adult Education-funded tour through Queensland, reading and talking about Australian poetry to country audiences. Most of those who came to listen were teachers and school students, since there was little interest in Australian writing unless it was set in examination syllabuses. On the whole the audiences were polite about most of the poetry I read, but they sat up when I read from Kath's work. It was not just the novelty of hearing an Aboriginal poet's work, but the force of the work itself which cut through to them.

> *Let none tell me the past is wholly gone.*
> *Now is so small a part of time, so small a part*
> *Of all the race-years that have moulded me.*

When I read that poem, "The Past", the first firm datings of Aboriginal sites to pre-glacial times had only just become public with the work of Mulvaney and Joyce on the Kenniff Cave in the Carnarvon Range. Those "thousand thousand campfires in the forest" which were in Kath's blood kindled a kind of shudder in the audience in themselves, but the poem itself provided that authentic shiver of response which poetry can give.

I read "Understand, Old One" and that shiver came again:

> *Strongly I feel your presence very near*
> *Haunting the old spot, watching*
> *As we disturb your bones. Poor ghost,*
> *I know, I know you will understand.*
> *What if you came back now*
> *To our new world, the city roaring*
> *There on the old peaceful camping place*
> *Of your red fires along the quiet water?*

This poem, with its ending:

> *Your duty to your race*
> *Was with the simple past, mine*
> *Lies in the present and the coming days*

seems like a kind of vow taken, a vow which Kath has carried out ever since.

I read them "Then and Now":

> *Now I have dress, now I have shoes:*
> *"Isn't she lucky to have good job?"*
> *Better when I had only a dillybag,*
> *Better when I had nothing but happiness.*

But the sharpest and funniest of the poems is "No More Boomerang". That poem always made audiences half-laugh, half-wince:

> *No more boomerang*
> *No more spear;*
> *Now all civilized –*
> *Colour-bar and beer*

with its hard-hitting final verse:

> *Lay down the woomera*
> *Lay down the waddy.*
> *Now we got atom-bomb,*
> *End* every*body.*

The point didn't need driving home in those terrifying days of the sixties.

In poems like these she proved again her capacity as critic of white civilisation as well as her capacity as speaker for her people. In poems like "Gifts" she employed her sardonic sense of fun:

> *"I will bring you the still moonlight on the lagoon,*
> *And steal for you the singing of all the birds;*
> *I will bring down the stars of heaven to you,*
> *And put the bright rainbow into your hand"*

sings the poetic lover.

> *"No," she said, "bring me treegrubs."*

That poem could be read as a rebuke to the critics too – those who held up before her the romantic traditions of English poetry, and demanded she give up the practical politics of her fight for her people's survival. But the critics complacently failed to see the point.

THE POETRY • 177

The two strands of change in Australia at the time were the new ascendancy of overseas-based standards of academic critical and canonical theory on literary matters which was shifting us back to English priorities from a brief rebellion after the betrayals of the Second World War, and an equally novel beginning of recognition that we could no longer go on seeing ourselves as an enclave of Europeans so far from a home that was growing less and less relevant to our reality. They were coming into sharp collision in the later sixties. Kath's work was deeply relevant to all this. I came back from that six-week Queensland tour with a new insight into her work, and respect for its bearing.

In fact, there were few of her poems that could be judged failures, once they were read aloud. There was instant communication, whether in agreement or antagonism. Poetry, in its beginnings, is oral. There's a special art in writing so as to make effectual statement, as well as effectual poem. Many of the other poems I read, from white Australian writers, failed obviously to make their point. Clusters of consonants, poor rhythmical communication and lack of consideration of breath-spaces can't be concealed in reading.

When a poet has something urgent, deeply felt, to say, those formal requirements can go hang, for the poem takes its own way and looks after itself. So a good story-teller, such as Maureen Watson, can hold an audience in the same way as the strongest of Kath's poems do; the words arouse feeling, because that is where they start. Formal correctness is a very small part of the communication that is real poetry.

There was no doubt, in my reading tour, whose poems made the most immediate impact of the evenings, not only because of the novelty of hearing a voice so unexpected and so demanding. No critical analysis can predict such effects and no formal perfection can evoke it.

The oral poet, such as Kath is, can use song-rhythms to make a point, to reach the hearer's own rhythms of breath and heart-beat.

Lay down the stone axe,
Take up the steel,
And work like a nigger

> *For a white-man meal.*
>
> …
>
> *Black hunted wallaby*
> *White hunt dollar;*
> *Whitefella witch-doctor*
> *Wear dog-collar.*
> ("No More Boomerang")

There is a bite and a rhythm about that which, read aloud, goes past the comic aspect into the heart of audience response. The collection *My People* (1970) has new narrative and dramatic poems which add a further angle of interest and variety to Kath's work. "Tribal Justice", in which a disobedient tribal member is punished by death, is rather marred by a switch between speech forms ("That fellow 'plenty bad', agreed an old pinaroo" in one verse, and "We will hold the spirit rites, we will find out./Let Darg do his magic to see who made the drought" in the next verse) so that comic and serious clash with discordant effect. "Jarri's Love Song" is an entirely comic tale, to "make camp laugh", and certainly succeeds from the reader's point of view.

> *Gecko fella, he got two tails* [sings the exultant lover]
> *But I… got… Nona.*
> *Frog he only got other frog*
> *But I… got… Nona.*
> *Gwoon got Weela with big hind part,*
> *She got seven kids before he start,*
> *Grey old Yundi got withered old Yan,*
> *But I… got… Nona.*

The much longer verse "Community Rain Song" is a much more ambitious and onomatopoeic attempt at interpreting the drought-breaking chant of the camp and the answering arrival of the storm. It is another oral poem which really needs to be acted and chanted rather than read. With its successive stages of response to the rain, with the camp's "community playabout" accompanied by the old men's "strange words of magic-making!" and lost "rain-words from ancestral times", the rain-dance and song, the coming of the "rainbird" (the channel-billed cuckoo), then the frogs croaking, the plover calling, the sound of the wind, the thunder accompanied by the answers from the camp, the climax in which all the strange calls mingle as the lightning and rain arrive, the poem or chant is the poet's attempt to recreate a life which in fact she had scarcely known. It can't be judged on the page; it should be acted and chanted; but how authentic in fact it is can't be judged by an audience of white readers.

To me, at least, the early editions of *My People*, up to the 1990 edition, are rather spoiled by a rearrangement of poems from the previous books along with the newer additions, so that sequence is lost, and the prose pieces and the epigrammatic short "Verses" are uneven. There are personal poems, poems which use modern-day vernacular to tell legendary stories now lost, and much more conventional verses, such as "Return to Nature", in no clear relation to each other, but the edition published in 1990 makes some amends for the previous editions and does her work more justice.

But whatever its unevenness, and its mostly deliberate disregard of "formal rightness" in a literary canon imposed by a culture and a literature far from her own, Kath's work has been immensely effective. It is above all an oral achievement, its functions are to arouse and move, to attack and appeal, even to amuse, not to employ subtle sophistication. That was her aim, and it is there that her success has to be acknowledged. At a time when it was important to assert the desperate situation of Aborigines, the injustices they suffer, and their real qualities, she has done all that with eminent success.

White critical response has been uncertain, various, but mainly rather shameful. Though the poems have been represented in many anthologies, in her own country and overseas, it has not always been her best or most varied work that has been included, and its real bearing and importance has not often been emphasised. The *Oxford History of Australian Literature*, a rather prim attempt at setting a canon, dismisses her work and that of all other Aboriginal poets in a couple of distasteful lines. The *Penguin Literary History of Australia*, a bicentennial production, does better, remarking in a fairly confident manner that the critiques of her poetry for "indulging in juvenile rhythm and rhyme and unsophisticated clichés" were "parochial, and overlooked her achievement". It draws attention to her free verse, quoting from "The Past" and pointing out that her pioneering success was only part of her significance to Aboriginal literature: "her best verse stands on its own, independent of such external considerations". Other critics, such as Adam Shoemaker in his book *Black Words, White Page*, give more credit and consideration to her achievement and its background (a matter avoided by other commentators). With reservations over some of the verses, he remarks that "the denial that Noonuccal is a poet amounts to a disturbingly limited critical position"; and he quotes with approval a reviewer's judgment that "Kath Walker has no need of metaphorical paraphernalia. She has a subject...When so many poets are trying to write who fundamentally have nothing to say... *We Are Going* is on the whole a refreshing book." He also emphasises the oral nature of her work and its added power when read aloud – its dramatic power.[3]

To sum up, the response of white critics and reviewers has sharply highlighted, for the most part, their own deficiencies of response. As she herself has always emphasised, the poems were written for her people, for their hopes of a future and their appalling treatment by their colonial and post-colonial invaders. That, not any attempt to rival white poets on their own ground, has been the point of the poems. To review them as though in fact they were an attempt to ape their colonists, is an avoidance tactic; to fail to comment on their real source and bearing is to misrepresent Kath Walker and her work entirely.

Since the appearance of *My People*, Kath – now Oodgeroo of the Noonuccal – has not published much verse. The verse travelogue written on her visit to China in 1984, published jointly by Jacaranda Press and the International Culture Publishing Corporation and printed in the People's Republic of China in 1988, is the only new collection.

Its sixteen verses, with an autobiographical introduction and a foreword by Manning Clark, also a member of the visiting party, record an experience which Clark called "like seeing a great work of art". For Manning himself, "it was the renewal of a hope I had entertained ever since my undergraduate days in Melbourne that humanity had a capacity for better things". Kath, now under her name of Noonuccal, "began to sparkle," wrote Manning; "she bubbled with excitement."

The new poems were, as he wrote, "a continuation of the themes which inform all her poetry – the wrongs the white people committed against her people, and her longing for a world in which those cruelties and barbarisms have disappeared off the face of the earth." That hope had been expressed in her first book, in "A Song of Hope":

Look up, my people,
The dawn is breaking,
The world is waking
To a new bright day,
When none defame us
No restriction tame us,
Nor colour shame us,
Nor sneer dismay.

Time hadn't changed that hope; and in this old culture she thought she saw renewal, as well as hospitality and beauty, art and faith in the present and future.

The poems are all free-verse, mostly simple descriptions of the sights the party were shown, and her own reaction to them. They turned out to have been naive, alas, when even before their publication in Australia tyranny and tragedy overtook her dream. But in 1984, when she had seen China for the first time, Tienanmen Square was peaceful, and she read it as welcoming her and the other visitors.

It would not have been like her to fail to respond to any promise of "a new bright day"; and if the verses stand now as a poignant reminder of hopes betrayed, they stand also as a record of a personality, and a poetry, that has never been daunted by the world's bitter contradictions of hope.

No survey of her work can fail to note its real effect. Even though so little may seem to have been achieved for Aborigines in the years since

1964, the grudging new respect for Aboriginal life, Aboriginal capacities, and Aboriginal art, owes far more to Oodgeroo Noonuccal's work whether as Kath Walker or as the descendant of her island people than has been acknowledged. It was, of course, not only in its effect on white readers and audiences that it will be remembered. Her own people knew of her, and were led and heartened by her work, from one side of Australia to the other. She was a legend; and among the people of the communities, reserves and fringes of the cities her fame put heart into people she could never have reached without the poems and their success. They were memorable, they were memorised and they will be remembered. Her work has vital things to say, as well as angry and funny and insulting and biting things. It has won its way against the white critics, the formalists, and the inventors of canons.

As the culture we have imported to this country wilts and changes under the pressures of reality, her poetry will outlast much that we have done. For poetry is real, and can survive. And Kath's poetry can take care of itself.

Judith Wright
Mongarlowe, 1992

Part Three Speeches

A Stranger in Tasmania
Third James McAuley Memorial Lecture
Delivered by Kath Walker in Hobart, 28 April 1982

I speak to you today as a stranger in Tasmania. Yours is the only state I have not worked in before. Indeed, I am more familiar with Harrisburg, Pennsylvania than Hobart and with Lagos, Nigeria than Launceston.

Despite my lack of familiarity with your land in a physical sense, I have been interested in Tasmania for many years. As an Aborigine, as a poet and as a conservationist, I have been moved and stirred by events in Tasmania.

I too make my home on an island and, as I flew south, I was awed by the vast distances involved. So few people in so much land!

Even fewer of my own Aboriginal people.

During 1976, Lyndall Ryan, a young student completing a doctorate (PhD) at Macquarie University, sent me a copy of her thesis on Aborigines in Tasmania. In that narrative I found understanding of the events that led to the destruction of traditional Aboriginal society in Tasmania.

I also found the Cape Barren Islanders and an awareness that the history of Tasmania was not much different to the mainland. As Lyndall says:

> The emergence of the Cape Barren Islanders was similar to that of other part-Aboriginal groups in South Eastern Australia. They were the result of interaction between European visitors and traditional Aboriginal groups in areas remote from "official" white control. The physical isolation allowed the islanders to develop a distinctive culture and lifestyle in much the same way that traditional Aboriginal society in Tasmania developed a separate but similar culture from the Aborigines on mainland Australia.

It was the same story with my tribe, the Noonuccal, on Stradbroke Island. Ultimately, we survived because of a degree of isolation from the mainland and because no one placed much economic value on the island at that time.

Often however when one mentions Tasmania in colleges and learned gatherings the world over, it is only known for the so called genocide of the Tasmanian Aborigines. Despite the persistence of the Cape Barren Islanders there can be no doubt that traditional Aboriginal society, a nation of four thousand people in about fifty tribes, was destroyed.

My unpublished poem "Oh Trugganner!" reveals my feelings when I had finished reading the Ryan thesis and it was indeed Lyndall Ryan who inspired me to write it.

Oh Trugganner!

Oh Trugganner,
I weep for you,
For Lanney and all your race,
As I read Ryan's damning thesis
After one hundred years.
Your desperate guerilla warfare
Failed to oust the white foe,
And spilt blood and tears
Freely flowed
Over your much loved land.
Your race
Was the trophy sought
By the "Christian, civilised" man
Who carried his depravities
Even beyond the grave.
Oh Trugganner,
I feel deep pain and sorrow
For the life he made for you.
What did you feel
When the foreign Doctor of Science
Stole like a thief in the night to the morgue
To cut from his body
Lanney's not yet cold head and his hands
In the name of "Christian" science?

Oh Trugganner,
What did your dreamtime spirit feel
As it watched them take you after death
As a rare museum piece,
To stay forever
Under the rude stares
Of vulgar public gaze?
Oh Trugganner,
Destined to be
Not just the last of your race,
But a prized specimen for science too.
Oh Trugganner,
Let your restless spirit
Bring comfort to us all.

Give us wisdom and strength,
For we have not yet found ourselves
In this now alien land.
This land we thought was ours for ever,
Now peopled with racists,
Murderers, manipulators,
Who know too well the art
Of conquer, enslave, kill and destroy.
Oh Trugganner,
Let your spirit rise from the foreign museum
And walk with us in our grief.
In our once loved Native land,
The love that sustains us,
Is what our race was
Before the invaders came.
Oh Trugganner,
As you cried in the past,
So too now do your people cry
And have cried for the last two hundred years.

Oh Trugganner,
Will the dreamtime spirits of our race
One day rise with us
As they did with you,
To the whispering sounds of stalking feet
With our guns in our hands
And an ambush plan
The nullas, the spears and stones?
Or will we in servitude,
Die like you?
And will "modern" scientists rave and drool
Over our bones
As they "religiously" did
With Lanney and you?
Oh Trugganner!

This is not to say that Tasmania stands alone in the world on some roll of dishonour. Claude McKay, a black American poet who wrote during the Harlem movement of the 1920s detailed the brutality and fear his people suffered. Little did he realise that his call to arms would be used by Winston Churchill himself to persuade the American Congress to enter the Second World War.

I cannot read one of his poems without thinking of the Tasmanians' fighting their desperate resistance and the remnant, dying, one by one, after being herded to Flinders Island – out of sight and out of mind.

> If we must die, let it not be like hogs,
> hunted and penned in an inglorious spot,
> while round us bark the mad and hungry dogs,
> making their mock at our accursed lot.
>
> If we must die, O let us nobly die,
> So that our precious blood may not be shed
> in vain; that even the monsters we defy
> shall be constrained to honour us, though dead!

> Like men we'll face the murderous cowardly pack,
> pressed to the wall, dying, but fighting back!

So it seems that Tasmania is not so very different from the rest of Australia and indeed from the world.

What is particularly sad to me, however, is that there could be no established Tasmanian Aboriginal poet to speak to you tonight. Instead you chose me, a stranger from the mainland, chosen because there is no representative of a people who had lived for more than twenty thousand years in this land.

It is the history of those twenty thousand years that I now wish to consider. Remains of mankind have been found to be forty thousand years old on the mainland but it has only been recently that remains of Aboriginal man from twenty thousand years ago have been discovered here.

Fraser Cave is the most southerly discovery of ancient man in the world. Here, in the Franklin Valley, Aborigines who crossed the land bridge from the mainland lived with a polar icepack only a thousand miles to the south and glaciers on nearby mountains.

To give you some perspective, mankind only drew those famous paintings in Spanish caves ten thousand years later. Here I stand, a representative of a people who occupied this land twenty thousand years before the descendants of those Spanish cave dwellers settled here. Suddenly I do not feel so much the stranger.

Although I too have European—yes, even Spanish—blood, I also am an Aborigine and I wonder how much of an identification with this land the descendants of the Europeans have developed in the last two hundred years.

There can be no doubt that the first European settlers found the land exceedingly strange and harsh. Lyndall Ryan states in her conclusion that

> The problem of the European and his inability to understand himself has always amazed and concerned the Aborigines. From first settlement Aborigines exclaimed at the senseless brutality of European society, the excesses of authoritarian control and the drive for conformity. Indeed Aboriginal society presented a challenge to long-held beliefs of concepts of man's soul and his relationship to the land. While Aborigines also thought that their society was superior to the invader's, they also understood that there would never be an opportunity to become part of the European, while the latter held "strange" ideas about them.
>
> In Aboriginal eyes the European may have had a superior technology but he used this technology in a senseless obliteration of a landscape he did not understand. To Aborigines therefore Europeans are a shallow people who are in a constant fear not only of the people whose land they have appropriated, but of the land itself. They are also afraid of external forces who will in turn expropriate their ill-gotten gains.

Judith Wright in her family history, *The Cry for the Dead*, details the life of her ancestors in the harsh new land. She describes the death and destruction of Aboriginal tribes which swiftly followed. Finally she describes the destruction of the land itself, the changes in forest cover and water courses and the hideous losses occasioned by over-grazing. Time and time again the balance was broken and the land struck back at the invaders.

Judith quotes William Forster, a squatting pioneer and premier of New South Wales (and, incidentally, occasional poet):

> 'Tis thus – a fatal race – where'er we go
> some phase of fitful tragedy appears.
> We strew the earth with murder, crime and woe…
> We pave our path with terror, blood and tears…

> Thus with whatever good
> our conquest brings, or seems to bring,
> perpetual evil mingles or conspires.
> Pale death and ruin round our footsteps spring,
> And desolation dogs our civilized desires.

Incidentally, the poem was addressed not to an Aborigine but to a kangaroo.

Judith described the destruction of the landscape caused by her farming family in the poem "Eroded Hills" published in the early 1960s:

> These hills my father's father stripped;
> and, beggars to the winter wind,
> they crouch like shoulders naked and whipped –
> humble, abandoned, out of mind.
>
> Of their scant creeks I drank once
> and ate sour cherries from old trees
> found in their gullies fruiting by chance.
> Neither fruit nor water gave my mind ease.
>
> I dream of hills bandaged in snow,
> their eyelids clenched to keep out fear.
> When the last leaf and bird go
> let my thoughts stand like trees here.

Again, in her poem "Old House", she records the destruction of the Aboriginal tribe on her great-great-grandfather's vineyard and ultimately, with their passing, the changes in the land.

> Where now outside the weary house the pepperina,
> that great broken tree, gropes with its blind hands
> and sings a moment in the magpie's voice, there he stood once,
> that redhaired man my great-great-grandfather,
> his long face amiable as an animal's,
> and thought of vines and horses.
> He moved in that mindless country like a red ant,

running tireless in the summer heat among the trees –
the nameless trees, the sleeping soil, the original river –
and said that the eastern slope would do for a vineyard.

In the camp by the river they made up songs about him,
songs about the waggons, songs about the cattle,
songs about the horses and the children and the woman.
These were a dream, something strayed out of a dream.
They would vanish down the river, but the river would flow on,
under the river-oaks the river would flow on,
winter and summer would burn the grass white
or red like the red of the pale man's hair.
In the camp by the river they made up those songs
and my great-great-grandfather heard them with one part of
   his mind.

And in those days
there was one of him and a thousand of them,
and in these days none are left –
neither a pale man with kangaroo-grass hair
nor a camp of dark singers mocking by the river.
And the trees and the creatures, all of them are gone.
But the sad river, the silted river,
under its dark banks the river flows on,
the wind still blows and the river still flows.
And the great broken tree, the dying pepperina,
clutches in its hands the fragments of a song.

And still today the land strikes back. And where my people would move on to give the land a chance to heal itself, the victims stay and mourn their loss of material possessions wondering why they and not others were unlucky.

Len Watson, an Aboriginal activist from Queensland discussed the European Australian relationship with land.

Land rights would seem to be in Australia the thing that excites white people like the sexual threat does to white people in America. I think they have the feeling that they are strangers here, which they are. They can't live on the land, they've got to use all their technology to help them live there and even then you get things like the flood in Brisbane or bushfires down in Tasmania.

Often when I speak to gatherings like this about the past, some white people tell me that they are consumed by guilt and resentment about actions over which they had no control. A young white woman, Elizabeth Smith, once wrote a poem in response to a speech of mine.

> Black mother
> you stand there on the stage, the spotlight white
> black eyes flashing – hands on hips –
> condemning me.
> Your anger flows and sparks in vicious words
> your rage strikes sparks of anguish from your black friends.
> They howl your anger back at you
> in words of black righteousness
> while I the only white one here
> howl also
> but not in anger.
> I howl in fear and sorrow.
> Black woman,
> do not hate me
> because I am white
> and free
> and guilty.

Please understand that it is not guilt and fear I try to arouse. Guilt is the most useless of human emotions. It paralyses thought and action and can most surely turn to hate.

But I must also stress that it is not enough to simply say that this occurred a hundred years ago – that what is done is done – that it is not our responsibility. It was men of the past who murdered and poisoned with gun and arsenic flour. But black babies are still dying today. Men of the past stole my people's land but few Aborigines today own any land.

Dr H.C. Coombs as chairman of the Federal Council for Aborigines reported that:

> An Aboriginal baby born today has a much better than average chance of being dead within two years. If it does survive it has a much better than average chance of suffering from sub-standard nutrition to a degree likely to handicap it in physical and mental potential, and in resistance to disease. It is likely to suffer from a wide range of diseases, particularly respiratory infections, gastroenteritis and eye infections.
>
> If it reaches teenage it is likely to be ignorant of and lacking in sound hygiene habits, without vocational training, unemployed, maladjusted and hostile to society.
>
> If it reaches adult age it is likely to be lethargic, irresponsible and above all poverty stricken – unable to break out of the iron cycle of poverty, ignorance, malnutrition, social isolation and antagonism. If it happens to be a girl it is likely to conceive a baby at an age when her contemporary in the white world is screaming innocent adulation at some pop star. She will continue to have babies every twelve to eighteen months until she dies of exhaustion.
>
> And so the wheel will turn.

Dr Coombs goes on further to say:

> It has been proven that children growing up in a poverty-stricken background, as many Aboriginal children do, will be eighteen months behind the others when they get to school and will never catch up, but instead fall further behind.
>
> Every time a child goes to school in this situation you, the Australian people and governments, are extending the problems in our society for another sixty years.
>
> We are producing a race of cripples – children who will never be able to live normal lives, every one of whom will be a heavy cost to the states.
>
> Unless the vicious circle of paternalism, dependence and pauperism is broken soon the problem will become much more difficult, if not impossible to solve.

The first step on the road to solution is land rights. It is no exaggeration to say that land rights is the central issue in Aboriginal affairs today. My people, the length and breadth of Australia will tell you this, no matter what shade our skin or whether we hunt with spear or rifle; work on stations or in mining camps; are employed by state or federal governments; sit in parliament or in the dole queue. The first step is land rights.

Slowly (increasingly) the world is taking notice. International attention is being focused on Australia and the treatment of Aborigines and especially their lack of land rights.

Churches, of many denominations, are mobilising on the issue. In April 1979 an Aboriginal Treaty Committee was formed by white people who see the importance of supporters organising nationally to help Aboriginal people in their fight for self-determination. As Lorna Lippman pointed out:

> In the traditional society, each group of Aborigines had a close and permanent relationship to a clearly defined tract of land. This land was not only their source of livelihood, it was also their spiritual centre, the land of their ancestors and the source of their social cohesion.
>
> One of the principal causes of present day Aboriginal poverty is the fact that no recompense was made for land, their only economic asset which was stolen (by the white invaders) from them. This contrasts with the situation of indigenous peoples in other countries: in India the land reserves of the tribal Aboriginal people are inviolate; among Maoris the Treaty of Waitangi in 1850 established, in practice though not legally, their right in New Zealand to the full exclusive and undisturbed possession of their lands and estates, forests, fisheries and other properties.
>
> In 1946 the United States Congress set up the Indian Claims Commission to settle claims by Indians against the United States arising from the taking by the United States, whether as a result of a treaty or cession or otherwise, of lands owned or occupied by the claimant tribe or group without the payment for such lands of compensation agreed to by the claimant.
>
> To date over 200 million dollars has been paid out on land claims and this money forms one of the chief sources of capital, and therefore of autonomy, for the Indian tribes. The Canadian government has now taken steps to establish an Indian Claims Commission.

Initially, the Aboriginal Treaty Committee was composed of a handful of academics and people of letters. They now have over three thousand supporters. They have decided that the time has come for white Australians to press for a legal treaty agreement between the Aboriginal inhabitants of this country and the Australian government.

The treaty would give back land in every state plus a fixed share of the wealth that land produces, especially minerals. The treaty will protect the languages, laws and Aboriginal way of life, our dances, songs and culture.

My people call this treaty the *Makarrata* and I would urge all white Australians who want to do something to support Dr Coombs and Judith Wright and the other members of the committee in bringing pressure to bear on the Australian government.

This document is more important, has greater cultural significance, than any verse or writing that either James McAuley or I ever wrote.

The second Tasmanian issue which has aroused mainland Australians as well as interested conservationists throughout the world is, of course, the proposals to flood the Franklin and Gordon rivers. Why is it that Tasmania is doomed to international recognition for destruction?

Perhaps some feel that it is better to be known for infamous deeds than not to be known at all. After all UNESCO described the flooding of Lake Pedder as the greatest ecological tragedy since European settlement of Tasmania.

The Tasmanian southwest is the largest temperate wilderness left in Australia and one of only three left in the world. It is considered by many Australians to be part of our national heritage. Indeed it is on the register of the national estate.

The federal government has nominated the southwest for the World Heritage List while the Tasmanian government has asked that only the Southwest National Park be nominated. This is in my opinion inadequate as it presently excludes the catchment of the Franklin, Davey and lower Gordon rivers. I cannot really understand how any government can decide that part of a wilderness is a part of our world heritage while the remaining wilderness is not. If accepted the wilderness will be one of eighty natural and man-made features deemed worthy of international conservation. All of the eastern states of Australia are having energy shortage problems and solutions must be found that do not destroy what we have no right to destroy. Is every generation of Australians to pay for the stupidity, short-sightedness and greed of their forebears?

But it is not only the flooding and destruction of the wildlife, the forests and rainforests, the rivers, chasms and waterfalls, it will also mean the destruction of my own people's history. To some those ancient remains in Fraser Cave are merely dirty pitiful reminders of a time out of mind. To me, each chip of bone, each flint and tooth or spearhead are my people's history. Inside that limestone cave people were born and died, sang and laughed after a fine hunt, developed rituals and religion to explain life. They taught their young skills that would mean unending occupation of a harsh environment for nearly twenty thousand years.

And today a government would wash it all away. First the people, then the land. And with the land the memories of a unique time.

In conclusion, I would say that although I am a stranger among you, I care deeply about the future of your island. I care about the sort of world our grandchildren will inherit. They must be given the opportunity to understand something of the people who once lived in their wilderness.

As naturalist William Beebe said: "When the last individual of a race of living beings breathes no more, another heaven and another earth must pass before such a one can be again."

Custodians of the Land
Written by Oodgeroo and Kabul
Delivered by Oodgeroo at Griffith University, 22 April 1989
on the occasion of the award to her of Honorary Doctorate of Letters

Allow me to begin this address by expressing my sincere gratitude to the Griffith University for bestowing such an honour upon me. It represents a milestone in the history of this land, now known as Australia, for it recognises (belatedly though it be) the value of a most ancient earth culture to modern society.

To the Aboriginal people, the modern history of this land began two hundred years ago, when the sacred shores of my people became the dumping ground for the "undesirable elements" from the crowded and depleted lands and social order of Old England. Some of these castaways were perpetuators of inhuman and irrational studies in the evolution of species (including the human), who merrily continued their insane traditions of racial and class discrimination here. Naturally, the first to suffer under this fascism were the traditional owners and occupiers of Australia, the Aborigines.

There were many reasons why the colonists considered Aboriginal people to be lesser creatures than apes. There were the obvious things, like our nakedness and different standards of physical beauty, but there was also their greed-based refusal to give credence to and therefore comprehend a non European-earth-raping culture, which, through an ancient excellence in social engineering, was not only highly successful but superior to their own.

We "pagans", who had believed in and comfortably maintained our own strict "code of moral behaviour" for all our people for many thousands of years before the white man's culture was born, were soon to learn that the equivalent order, in their brave new world, was most sadistically maintained with the rabid and obsessive use of the infamous cat-o'-nine-tails whip.

We need not labour these things for the purpose of this event, except, perhaps, to take note and to remember that these basic living differences between the two cultures created a fundamental clash then, and the modern issue is one of diametrically opposed philosophies that continue to clash now. Blind prejudice to cultural difference is still being liberally indulged in today in this land known as Australia.

Australia is still being used as a dumping ground for many other world cultures. Unfortunately, instead of providing a bridge between Aborigines and European Australians, it merely adds to the rift. It must be clearly understood that the Aboriginal nation (yet to be recognised) has little or no enthusiasm for the so-called multicultural society of Australia, for it is unbelievable and a great indictment of European Australians that the Aboriginal people find themselves once again at the bottom of the Australian socioeconomic scale with regard to multiculturalism. In the multicultural case, we continually find ourselves firmly lacking in any priority of position on any "ethnic" shopping list. This is true in all areas, including theatre. But then again, one must never mention the selling off of the Aborigines' stolen lands to multinationals in the same breath as the expression "multiculturalism".

As a proud Aborigine, I have witnessed, among Asian and European peoples, the replanting of their grassroot cultures on my Aboriginal homeland, and I have seen only the continuation of prejudice and suffering for my people. Only the history of the European and English Australian, it seems, repeats itself over and over again in this, my country.

Modern Australia, however, does have the key to logical race relations, but white Australia is preventing it from happening. Firstly, it is prevented with egotistic insistence on assimilation for all other cultures, by implementing heavily weighted Anglo-Saxon educational methods and systems. Secondly, through refusing to acknowledge that traditional Anglo-Saxon estimations of what constitutes intelligence and criteria for assessing ability and achievement must be reshaped in order to recognise and include other aptitudes at grassroot level.

It is possible to rectify this situation with a sensible, fair and reasonable approach to education. Education departments must revise their out-of-date, mid-Victorian criteria. When tutors from other countries and Aboriginal elders from this country, through cultural exchange, are recognised and their true worth recognised in universities and schools, then we will have, and will be able to boast of, a truly multicultural society.

At present, however, when Aboriginal people "achieve" at a university or tertiary institution, they are forced to lead a double life. By day such a person is a replica of a white Australian, slightly – sometimes heavily – suntanned, who is taught to respect and accept the same Anglo-Saxon heroes as his or her peers; by night, a "real" person, with his or her own cultural identity. I have named this double existence "the super-hero syndrome".

There are many Aboriginal people in Australia leading this double existence who are irreparably damaged by the static they receive from their own families and communities for their achievements in the Anglo-Saxon world. Their strivings are seen as betrayal and psychologically ill. They are known to their people as "Jackys" and "Marys", or "coconuts", the definition being "brown on the outside, white on the inside". The reason for all this cattle dust is that the Australian heroes are all Anglo-Saxon, and if any Aboriginal student challenges this, she or he is frozen out of the education system until they learn to be "rational". Becoming "rational" of course means "agreeing to assimilate". It is this or become the black dropout, those Aboriginal subjects of innumerable university theses and government surveys, the conducting of which regularly provides non-Aboriginal students with their own degrees.

European Australians must let go of England. It is time to do just that. American universities are the leaders in providing cultural role models for students. The way to a "real" multicultural society in Australia is through providing relevant role models for our students. We must duplicate the American pattern, for it does work; I have seen it. Or must I, as an Aboriginal elder, advise Aboriginal students to seek higher education in America?

Australian educational institutions can and must lead the way in forcing parliaments to recognise these urgent needs. Concurrently, our universities must acknowledge and recognise the fact that their domineering and entrenched elitism still implements the mid-Victorian attitude of "survival of the white tribe at any cost" and is counterproductive to a racial equality of the future.

It is, therefore, both logical and imperative that this elitism be hastily dissolved. White Australians must accept that it is time for them to be the listeners and the learners. They must accept that Aboriginal and ethnic people have their own traditional and contemporary tutors, and they are available here and now. In short, let us learn and understand logical grassroot culture of *all races* – an exchange where *all races* stand equal unto each other. Then and only then can there ever be a true multicultural Australia.

But let us consider for one moment the reality of what is happening in this world today in racial terms. There can be no doubt that the grassroot peoples of the Southern Hemisphere are embarking on a natural course of balance. This is to be expected and accepted (if we are clever), after hundreds of years of evil and ugly colonial yoke. There can also be no doubt that in some cases, as in South Africa, where the rule of a fanatical white minority, using Christianity as their motive, anthropology as their weapon and technology as their alibi against the traditional land owners, can end only in the most dreadful letting of blood, the like of which we have not seen since the last world war. I need not spell out the similar patterns emerging in South America. Fiji, however, is a very real beginning of the Southern Hemisphere of the future, if indeed there is to be a future for humankind under the umbrellas of nations who have at their heads fascist, nationalist boys who long to play with atomic toys.

Reading between the lines, Vanuatu, New Caledonia, New Guinea, and the Torres Strait Islands will surely follow the trend that Fiji has set in the push for grassroot autonomy, the natural balance.

The Anglo-Saxon world is shrinking; the grassroot worlds are reawakening from the effects of the colonial brutality. Where, then, does this leave seventh-generation Australians? At present we have a situation where grassroot peoples are on one side and European and ethnic races in this country are on the other side. The predicament can easily lead to placing the Australian-born seventh-generation community in a proverbial hotseat with regard to their perpetuation of cruelty, apathy and violence towards the Aborigines, the grassroot custodians of this land.

Bet let us make no hasty mistake when pondering this natural, long-awaited and coming shift of the Southern Hemisphere. Grassroot autonomy in every sense, that is, economically, culturally, socially and psychologically, is the only path to racial harmony. And on this basis it is time to start drawing up a blueprint for the global village of the future. We of the Pacific must provide the working model of socioeconomic equality for all peoples.

There is no doubt that education, correctly applied, can meet our future needs in this, and recognition and acceptance of the true value of grassroot and ethnic teaching methods is a step in the right direction for an evenly balanced future.

This blueprint should begin, perhaps, with the establishing of the armed neutrality of Australia. We have lost too many sons and daughters to the war games their war lords play. An armed but neutral major power in the Southern Hemisphere must cause new thought, which will lead to new socioeconomic reform. New generations of non-violent, non-racist, non-conformers will have the opportunity to uphold peace in the Southern Hemisphere. The dumping of war lords from other countries onto our shores, be they English, Japanese, South African, Chinese, German or any other, will turn the Australian multicultural dream of the nineties into the nightmare of the next century.

As I have previously stated, Australian history books assert that Aboriginal and Australian history began in 1770. Our children's textbooks still imply this nonsense. We are also urged to believe that our Aboriginal political existence began on 27 May 1967, with the referendum.

Australian archaeologists are just now beginning to discover what Aboriginal people have always known. We have been here for a very, very long time, and, furthermore, much to the disgust of some, have no intention of going away, even in the face of attempted genocide.

Our ancient history is locked in a cultural memory, which in turn is locked in the Alcheringa, or, as it has been renamed (incidentally, without our permission), the Dreamtime. Non-Aboriginal Australians will eventually receive this history, for it will be translated into forms that all can understand by the Aboriginal people themselves. This not only for our benefit, though we sorely need it, but also for the benefit of all races – this in spite of the fact that the present Constitution of Australia gives little to Aborigines in terms of cultural survival.

In the meantime, however, we must rely on our white friends to report our history from their perspective. Two educative books stand out in my mind – belatedly written, but of great importance. They should be used as textbooks at all levels of education from universities down. They are: *The Law of the Land,* by Henry Reynolds, and *The Fatal Shore*, by Robert Hughes.

These books are but two of a great mass of research emerging that will, in my view, change the very way this country thinks. In my opinion, they have the potential to represent the beginning of a new and great Australian philosophy – one that has no time or patience for the convenient prejudices of the self-indulgent and illegitimate squattocracy that has been the very meaning of the word "Australia" for two hundred years. This new thought means most to the *young* Australians and is bringing them fascination with and pride in Aboriginal culture and less shame and guilt in their own. These two books also symbolise, for me, the great anger and bitterness that young Australians are feeling against an education system that has deliberately kept them blinded to the truth of the so-called "bringing of civilisation" to this land. *Aboriginal activists will not forge change* and redress injustices as much as the young *white Australian* people, who are already outraged at being isolated from the deep wells of wisdom that dot the landscape of an ancient and profound culture.

The authors of these two books I have mentioned are in no way anarchists or revolutionaries; they are as academic, level-headed and analytical as their families always hoped they would be. They have simply begun a sensible and logical step in this country's history by exposing past untruths, discovering the reality, assessing this and restating the facts intelligently.

I cannot praise these and other works of this kind too highly. Perhaps, when such ideas are introduced into our education systems, the present-day students may encourage their, what I call, "mentally constipated adults" to also peruse these works.

You have heard the Aboriginal point of view. Before summing up I would like to introduce you to a non-Aboriginal point of view… Last year you honoured Judith Wright McKinney with a doctorate. She is, in my opinion, the greatest poet of her generation. Here is the poem she wrote in her attempt to sum up white Australia. What she has to say is worthy of your consideration.

Two Dreamtimes
(For Kath Walker)

Kathy my sister with the torn heart,
I don't know how to thank you
for your dreamtime stories of joy and grief
written on paperbark.

You were the one of the dark children
I wasn't allowed to play with –
riverbank, campers, the wrong colour,
(I couldn't turn you white.)

So it was late I met you,
late I began to know
they hadn't told me the land I loved
was taken out of your hands.

Sitting all night at my kitchen table
with a cry and a song in your voice,
your eyes were full of the dying children,
the blank-eyed taken women,

the sullen looks of the men who sold them
for rum to forget the selling,
the hard rational white faces
with eyes that forget the past.

With a knifeblade flash in your black eyes
that always long to be blacker,
your Spanish-Koori face
of a fighter and singer,

arms over your breast folding
your sorrow in to hold it,
you brought me to you some of the way
and came the rest to meet me,

over the desert of red sand
came from your lost country
to where I stand with all my fathers,
their guilt and righteousness.

Over the rum your voice sang
the tales of an old people,
their dreaming buried, the place forgotten…
We too have lost our dreaming.

We the robbers robbed in turn,
selling this land on hire-purchase;
what's stolen once is stolen again
even before we know it.

If we are sisters, it's in this –
our grief for a lost country,

the place we dreamed in long ago,
poisoned now and crumbling.

Let us go back to that far time,
I riding the cleared hills,
plucking blue leaves for their eucalypt scent,

hearing the call of the plover,
in a land I thought was mine for life.
I mourn it as you mourn
the ripped length of the island beaches,
the drained paperbark swamps.

The easy Eden-dreamtime then
in a country of birds and trees
made me your shadow-sister, child,
dark girl I couldn't play with.

But we are grown to a changed world:
over the drinks at night
we can exchange our separate griefs,
but yours and mine are different.

A knife's between us. My righteous kin
still have cruel faces.
Neither you nor I can win them,
though we meet in secret kindness.

I am born of the conquerors,
you of the persecuted.
Raped by rum and an alien law,
progress and economics,

are you and I and a once-loved land
peopled by tribes and trees;
doomed by traders and stock exchanges,
bought by faceless strangers.

And you and I are bought and sold,
our songs and stories too
though quoted low in a falling market
(publishers shake their heads at poets).

Time that we shared for a little while,
telling sad tales of women
(black or white at a different price)
meant much and little to us.

My shadow-sister, I sing to you
from my place with my righteous kin,
to where you stand with the Koori dead,
"Trust none – not even poets."

The knife's between us. I turn it round,
the handle to your side,
the weapon made from your country's bones.
I have no right to take it.

But both of us die as our dreamtime dies.
I don't know what to give you
for your gay stories, your sad eyes,
but that, and a poem, sister.

In summing up, I would like to restate that a multicultural society can only successfully occur in this country when seventh-generation Australians recognise the Aboriginal culture. No change will or can occur until the theft of Aboriginal land and the attempted enslaving and slaughter are redressed and compensated. This Aboriginal land will never accept and will always be alien to any race who dares try enslave her. Aborigines will always be the custodians of their traditional lands, regardless of any other enforced law system, for the land is our Mother. We cannot own her; she owns us!

Beyond Terra Nullius, the Lie
Written by Oodgeroo and Denis Walker
Delivered by Oodgeroo at Queensland University of Technology, 1992
on the occasion of the award to her of Honorary Doctorate of Letters

Terra Nullius was a legal lie used by the invading forces of the British to deny the legal rights of the indigenous people of this country, now called Australia.

This legal lie of Terra Nullius has been used right up to and until the High Court of Australia handed down its decision on the now famous Mabo case. All previous claims at law by the indigenous people had, up until that time, foundered on the rocks of that legal lie of Terra Nullius.

Now that the highest court in this land has recognised the pre-existing legal rights of the indigenous people, many forms of settlement of dispute of their territories and their law/lore must be made.

Settlements must be made by way of treaties at all local levels through the blood lines back to their territories and agreed to by their elders in council at their local level. Legislation, be it state or federal, will not be sufficient, nor will decisions made by the High Court. Such actions as stated are impositions and, as such, would continue to deny true justice to the indigenous people of this country.

Settlements of disputes at law/lore involving indigenous people and their territories should be considered by their elders in council at the local level and those considerations be given equal weightage with the invaders' law in resolving such disputes, to the extent that conditions regarding environment and remunerations need to be agreed to before settlement can take place.

Recognition of the indigenous people's territorial and legal rights can only be justifiably dealt with by way of treaty mechanism. Anything else is an imposition and will merely water down the lie of Terra Nullius.

Because of the genocidal policies arising out of Terra Nullius, the lie, a great deal of disruption has taken place with the indigenous people and their territories. They will need immediate resources to allow them to restructure and redefine themselves in order for them to settle all outstanding matters.

Embodied in this process is the urgent necessity to recognise justice as natural law/lore. The invaders' law defines this natural law thus: "Natural law is God's law and is superior to man made laws."

Indigenous people have had to live through and survive the holocaust of the genocidal policies arising out of the legal lie of Terra Nullius for over 200 years. To delay any further is to continue to deny the indigenous people of this country true and equal justice.

The ongoing problems within the spheres of indigenous peoples' existence such as high rates of imprisonment, high infant mortality rates, deaths in custody, breakdown of extended family units, substance abuse, domestic violence, etc are all components making up the situation that constitutes an iron cycle which we have yet to break. The "piecemeal" approaches of the past have not worked. In the main these "piecemeal" attempts have been received as impositions that have been rejected.

In conclusion, last but by no means least is the spirituality of the indigenous people of this country. Their spirituality is *not* a religion. It is tied firmly to the spirit of their Earth Mother who created all living things. Their sentries the rocks, their sea, land and air spirits... are very much a part of their culture as is their philosophy which states: "We cannot own the land for the land owns us."

The constitution of Australia was written to meet the needs of the invading English "haves" at the expense of the "have nots".

It is time to shred the present English constitution and replace it with an Australian constitution which meets the needs of *all* races now living in this country.

Writers of Australia, "I dips me lid"
Goossens Lecture delivered at the Sydney Opera House, 9 June 1993
Oodgeroo's last major public speech

As a very proud member of the Aboriginal race of Australia I have chosen to take you down memory lane with me and to explain how I, as an uncivilised pagan of the Noonuccal clan of Minjerribah, North Stradbroke Island, coped with the English language in the civilised schools of the invaders of this my country.

Time does not permit me to cover all the fields of Australian writers so I intend to speak about the theme I am most conversant with, namely poetry. However, the playwrights, the novelists and historians are indeed worthy of mention. Again, I can mention but a few who come to mind owing to the lack of time. Those whom I do not mention, I hope will understand and forgive me if I have not called their names. Three playwrights immediately come to mind: David Williamson, Jack Davis and, now departed, Kevin Gilbert. Novelists and poets John Manifold, Tom Shapcott, Bruce Dawe, Elizabeth Jolley, Dorothy Hewett, Nancy Cato, Mudrooroo Narogin (also known as Colin Johnson), Archie Weller. And among historians who are worthy of our attention for they have really taken us into a field that had not been discovered until about 1988: Robert Hughes (*The Fatal Shore*), Bruce Elder (*Blood on the Wattle*), Henry Reynolds (*The Law of the Land*), Bill Rosser (*Up Rode the Troopers*). To all the writers of Australia, let me say "Well done" and, to quote C.J. Dennis, "I dips me lid".

And now, a walk down memory lane. As a schoolgirl at Dunwich State School my first introduction to poems was a poem called "Vitaï Lampada" written during the English colonialist era, and in English; and it was compulsory reading. Now, when I was introduced to this poem I was very interested. He's talking about cricket and he's talking about war and I really thought that cricket was a sort of war dance they went into before they went into war to kill or be killed. Here's a few lines from the "Vitaï Lampada":

> There's a breathless hush in the close tonight—
> Ten to make, and the match to win —
> A bumping pitch and a blinding light,
> An hour to play and the last man in.
> And it's not for the sake of a ribboned coat,
> Or the selfish hope of a season's fame,
> But his Captain's hand on his shoulder smote —
> "Play up! play up! and play the game!"

Now that sounds all right, that sounds like cricket to me. But then the second verse threw me because it goes something like this:

> The sand of the desert is sodden red,
> Red with the wreck of the square that broke;
> The Gatling's jammed and the Colonel dead,
> And the regiment blind with dust and smoke.
> The river of death has brimmed his banks,
> And England's far and Honour a name,
> But the voice of a schoolboy rallies the ranks:
> "Play up! play up! and play the game!"

"Vitaï Lampada" for what it's worth. And I don't know… I'm not quite sure what Vitaï Lampada means. And it was strange because further to this came a poem called "Home", and it went something like this:

> Far, far away across the world
> A fine old island lies;
> Its seas, they say, are green and grey,
> And blue and grey its skies.
> There castles are, and battlefields,
> Old inns and bowling greens;

Great abbeys and the darksome tower,
And tombs of kings and queens.
There Britons lived, and Norse and Danes,
And men who came from Rome—
Grandfather lived there long ago—
Grandfather calls it—*home.*

So *I* belong to *it,* you see,
And *it* belongs to mine and me,
So *I* shall call it—*home.*

I never did find out for a long time what "home" was. I found out belatedly that it happened to be England, which shows I was definitely educated, you would say?

Then came the works of Shakespeare and one poem we had to learn by heart, and we did, and we of the Noonuccal tribe found it very interesting because the last line of this little ditty was very interesting to us and so we did a bit of mucking around with it with the Aboriginal language. But here it is:

When icicles hang by the wall
And Dick, the shepherd, blows his nail,
And Tom bears logs into the hall,
And milk comes frozen home in pail,
When blood is nipped and ways be foul
Then nightly sings the staring owl, Tu-who;
"Tu-whit, tu-woo" a merry note,
While greasy Joan doth keel the pot.

Now we changed that last line because it looked rather boring to us. We thought we'd jumpy it up a bit. With the Aboriginal word of the Noonuccal Tribe of Stradbroke Island, we changed this to:

While greasy Joan doth geel at the pot.

Now the word "geel" is not to be used in public, but what I can say to you is that—this is a hallowed place, this is the Opera House—and so all I can say is that the word "geel" written in translation into the English rhymes with "hiss". So much for Shakespeare!

Now, the last scene of Othello intrigued me, you know:

> Soft you; a word or two before you go.
> I have done the State some service.

Then he goes on and on. He'd just killed Desdemona, she's lying there looking very sexless, blood all over her, and when he says:

> Set you down this;
> And say, besides, that in Aleppo once,
> Where a malignant and a turbaned Turk
> Beat a Venetian and introduced the state,
> I took by the throat the circumcised dog,
> And smote him thus.

"But you see ere I kill thee," etc. Now this intrigued me because, I felt, why did he have to mention the man being circumcised? Was he attacking the custom of the Jewish people by mentioning the circumcised dog? And if he was he ought to be downright ashamed of himself because in my opinion he was a [?] racist. I didn't like that one very much, that part. However, I've seen they've changed it lately.

And then came the early Australian writers and the one that I found very interesting to me was a poem, Mary Gilmore's interpretation of colonialism.

> I'm old
> Botany Bay;
>
> Stiff in the joints,
> Little to say

I am he
Who paved the way,
that you might walk
at your ease today;

I was the conscript
Sent to hell
To make in the desert
The living well;

I bore the heat,
I blazed the track—
Furrowed and bloody
Upon my back.

I split the rock;
I felled the tree:
the Nation *was*
Because of me.
Old Botany Bay…

I think Mary Gilmore did not like what they were doing to the environment of Botany Bay and that was her objection to what they were doing. I don't think she was praising us, I think she was condemning us at that period of time.

And then came an introduction to another writer and I was quite happy about this writer because she was talking about her country and —oh, miracle of miracles—it had been my country too. And it went something like this:

I love a sunburnt country,
A land of sweeping plains,

Of ragged mountain ranges,
Of drought and flooding rains.
I love her far horizons,
I love her jewel-sea,
Her beauty and her terror—
The wide brown land for me!

And Dorothea Mackellar became one of my favourite poets because she was talking about my country as well as hers.

And then came another introduction to another poet when I was in my teens and I was quite amazed at this poet because (a) she was white, (b) she was a writer and (c) she cared so much that on riding out one day she saw what had happened to a bora ring and was really upset about it. In later years when I met Judith Wright she explained to me that as soon as she saw the damage done to that bora ring she turned her horse around, went home, sat down and wrote her now famous poem called "Bora Ring":

The song is gone; the dance
is secret with the dancers in the earth,
the ritual useless, and the tribal story
lost in an alien tale

Only the grass stands up
to mark the dancing-ring: the apple gums
posture and mime a past corroboree,
Murmur a broken chant.

The hunter is gone: the spear
is splintered underground; the painted bodies

a dream the world breathed sleeping and forgot.
The nomad feet are still.

Only the rider's heart
halts at a sightless shadow, an unsaid word
that fastens in the blood the ancient curse,
the fear as old as Cain.

She felt very unhappy about that very sad thing because she said she looked in vain for the Aboriginals and she knew that they'd all disappeared. They had been absolutely wiped out.

When I was up at Judith Wright's place writing my *Stradbroke Dreamtime* book I wrote that very famous story about Oodgeroo and I took it to her the first time and said "What do you think of this for a first draft?" Without a word she went to her library and she took down off the bookshelf her poems and then she turned to a page and said "Read that".

After I'd read it I was amazed because what I'd done in story form, Judith Wright had written in poem form long before she'd known Kath Walker the writer or the woman. I said "Judith, how did you know, how did you really know that it would be a woman who would come through the first from the Aboriginal world to be a poet?" She said something very beautiful. She said "You and I have been sisters in another Dreamtime a long, long time ago." And I've never forgotten her saying that. But here it is, she's called it "Canefields":

The coloured girl leans on the bridge,
folding her sorrow into her breast.
Her face is a dark and downward mirror
where her eyes look, and are lost.

The old land is marshalled under
the heavy regiment of green cane;
but by the lagoon the paperbarks
unroll their blank and tattered parchment,
waiting for some unknown inscription
which love might make in ink-dark water.

And in that water the great lily
sets her perfect dusk-blue petals
in their inherited order of prayer
around that blazing throne, her centre.
There time shall meet eternity
and her worship find its answer.

It's a most amazing thing that happened and very few people realise that's what Judith Wright had predicted. Then came the sixties and—miracle of miracles—Aboriginals were not only speaking English, they were actually writing it. And Kath Walker was the first poet through the field and I tried to analyse for myself what was this civilisation everyone was talking about, you know. I thought, everyone's telling me I should be civilised, and what this civilisation is all about, so I decided I would write a poem about my interpretation of civilisation. I called it "Civilisation". This has really been a poem that got me into a lot of trouble. A lot of people didn't like my interpretation of civilisation. So here it is:

Civilisation

We who came late to civilisation,
Missing a gap of centuries,
When you came we marvelled and admired,
But with foreboding.
We had so little but we had happiness,
Each day a holiday,
For we were people before we were citizens,
Before we were ratepayers,
Tenants, customers, employees, parishioners.
How could we understand white man's gradings,
Rigid and unquestioned,
Your sacred totems of Lord and Lady,
Highness and Holiness, Eminence, Majesty?
We could not understand

Your strange cult of uniformity,
This mass obedience to clocks, timetables.
Puzzled, we wondered why
The importance to you, urgent and essential,
Of ties and gloves, shoe-polish, uniforms.
New to us were jails and orphanages,
Rates and taxes, banks and mortgages.
We who had so few things, the prime things,
We had no policemen, lawyers, middlemen,
Brokers, financiers, millionaires.
So they bewildered us, all the new wonders,
Stocks and shares, real estate,
Compound interest, sales and investments.
Oh, we have benefited, we have been lifted
With new knowledge, a new world opened.
Suddenly caught up in white man's ways
Gladly and gratefully we accept,
For this is necessity.
But remember, white man,
If life is for happiness,
You too, surely, have much to change.

And so the critics were out with their sharp pens and their sharp claws.

Next came Jack Davis and Jack Davis and I were in the civil rights movement together and the FCAATSI movement and we were always trying to be good educators to educate our good white friends who stood with us in the FCAATSI movement and we'd get very tired after conferences and he would go to his beloved Western Australia and I would go down home to my beloved Stradbroke Island. One day he was sitting out—he'd go bush straight away, to think about and ponder over things. One day he said to me "You know, Kathie, I don't know whether we are very bad educators or the white people are slow learners." I think that's enough of that one.

But he was out another time and he was sitting there and he was thinking to himself "What would the Earth Mother think—the Rainbow Serpent who now sleeps at Ayers Rock—what would she do if she came back after the two hundred years of the invasion and saw the land and what had happened to this land and the desecration of it. He wondered what she would say about it and, he said, all of a sudden her voice came to him on the wind and, he said, "I grabbed for my pen and my paper" and he came up with "The First-Born".

> Where are my first-born, said the brown land, sighing:
> They came out of my womb long, long ago.
> They were formed of my dust—why, why are they crying
> And the light of their being barely aglow?
>
> I strain my ears for the sound of their laughter.
> Where are the laws and the legends I gave?
> Tell me what happened, you whom I bore after.
> Now only their spirits dwell in the caves.
>
> You are silent, you cringe from replying.
> A question is there, like a blow on the face.
> The answer is there when I look at the dying,
> At the death and neglect of my dark proud race.

I envy him writing that because I wish it were mine. I told him that time and time again. However, he says he'll give me permission to recite it any time I like. He says I can do it better than him, so fair enough.

So I'd like to now talk about some of the Aboriginal poets who came to the field. I'm very proud to tell you that, in this short period of thirty years since the FCAATSI movement, I'm proud to say that we have forty-two published poets in the field in the initial period of thirty years. That makes me feel very, very proud of my own people and, as it is the Year of the Indigene, as a salute to them, I'd like to read now some of the poems of our indigenous people.

The first one I'd like to introduce you to is Eva Johnson of South Australia. Eva Johnson's story is not a pretty one. She was taken off her mother — it was the civilising process that they entered into, the governments of that day. If you were born with a skerrick of white man's blood in you, you were ripped out of the arms of your full-blood mother and handed over to white people to rear, or missionaries. Eva grew up and all her life she went looking for her mother. Belatedly she found her and got on the first plane up to Darwin to find her mother. She was with her for a little time then she had to go back to work in Adelaide and a month later word came through that her mother had passed away: the end result of which is that Eva is a very, very bitter person and she feels that she has been robbed unnecessarily and for no reason whatsoever. Before she found her mother she wrote this poem. It's called "A Letter to My Mother".

> I not see you long time now, I not see you long time now
> White fulla bin take me from you, I don't know why
> Give me to Missionary to be God's child.
> Give me new language, give me new name
> All time I cry, they say — "that shame"
> I go to city down south, real cold
> I forget all them stories, my Mother you told
> Gone is my spirit, my dreaming, my name
> Gone to these people, our country to claim
> They gave me white mother, she give me new name
> All time I cry, she say — "that shame"
> I not see you long time now, I not see you long time now.

I grow as Woman now, not Piccaninny no more
I need you to teach me your wisdom, your lore
I am your Spirit, I'll stay alive
But in white fulla way, you won't survive
I'll fight for your land, for your Sacred sites
To sing and to dance with the Brolga in flight
To continue to live in your own tradition
A culture for me was replaced by a mission
I not see you long time now, I not see you long time now.

One day your dancing, your dreaming, your song
Will take me your Spirit back where I belong
My mother, the earth, the land—I demand
Protection from aliens who rule, who command
For they do not know where our dreaming began
Our destiny lies in the laws of White Man
Two Women we stand, our story untold
But now as our spiritual bondage unfold
We will silence this Burden, this longing, this pain
When I hear you, my Mother, give me my Name
I not see you long time now, I not see you long time now.

It speaks for itself. Incidentally most of the people in this book, the writers in this book, are still looking for their mothers. I was one of the lucky ones, I had my mother. I can't imagine what I'd do without my mother. Just as well I had my mother because I'd have been much more angry than what I am and I don't think Australia could handle me.

Colin Johnson, now called Mudrooroo Narogin, is another angry man who was taken and put in a home. He's got his family of nine. When he had written "Wild Cat Falling" and then tucked his tail between his legs and ran to the security of the Indian people and Buddhism because he didn't know anything about his own culture, when he came back he was very, very bitter and he's still very angry because when he came back I said "Colin I'll help you find your family for you" and he said "No, don't." I said "Why not?" and he said "Because when I was in jail I dreamed of what they'd be like." He said "I went from home detention place because I was supposed to be uncontrollable in the streets and all my family was all split up and they all went to different missions." And he said "Then I ran foul of the law and ended up in jail" and he said "When I was in jail I used to dream what they'd be like. He said "If you give me the reality it might spoil my dream." He still will not look for his family. And this is Colin Johnson's poem called "They Give Jacky Rights":

> They give Jacky rights,
> Like the tiger snake gives rights to its prey:
> They give Jacky rights,
> Like the rifle sights on its victim.
> They give Jacky rights,
> Like they give rights to the unborn baby,
> Ripped from the womb by its uncaring mother.
>
> They give Jacky the right to die,
> The right to consent to mining on his land.
> They give Jacky the right to watch
> His sacred dreaming place become a hole—
> His soul dies, his ancestors cry;
> His soul dies, his ancestors cry:
> They give Jacky his rights—
> A hole in the ground!
>
> Justice for all, Jacky kneels and prays;
> Justice for all, they dig holes in his earth;
> Justice for all, they give him his rights—
> A flagon of cheap wine to dull his pain,
> And his woman has to sell herself for that.

Justice for all, they give him his rights—
A hole in the ground to hide his mistrust and fear.
What can Jacky do, but struggle on and on:
The spirits of his Dreaming keep him strong!

Another angry young man.

Maureen Watson is well known for her storytelling and her poetry. Maureen Watson is one of these liberated people and she's going to spend the rest of her life, I think, trying to liberate all you women from these bad people called men. She's out to liberate all the women of the world. And this is her poem about it—it's called "Stepping Out".

I'm stepping out, don't mess about.
Don't tell me to be patient.
I've been wedded, enslaved, white washed, and saved,
But now, I'm liberated.
I've been patted, and moulded, and shaped, and scolded
And I learned real fast how to please 'em,
I "Yessir"ed, and "No Ma' am"ed,
I was cursed and damned,
And all for no good reason.
I've been put up, and I've been put down,
By folks who were black, white, yellow or brown.
Treated like I wasn't human, just a puppet, a token,
But I healed my hurts, 'cause for better or worse,
Black woman's got spirit that's never going to be broken.
Been labelled all my life,
Black, woman, mother and wife.
And their labels formed the bars of my prison,
But I've got to set free this person who's me.

'Cause now I've got a vision,
Their myths and lies are dead,
Not heaped on my head,
And their history is all outdated,
Different sex, different skin, can't change what's within,
'Cause now, I'm liberated,
And I'm stepping out, don't mess about,
Don't tell me to be patient,
No ifs or buts.
I don't walk, I strut,
'Cause now, I'm liberated.

Glory! And her wonderful poem that she writes, this "Memo to JC":

When you were down here JC and walked this earth,
You were a pretty decent sort of bloke,
Although you never owned nothing, but the clothes on your back,
And you were always walking round, broke.
But you could talk to people, and you didn't have to judge,
You didn't mind helping the down and out
But these fellows preaching now in your Holy name,
Just what are they on about?
Didn't you tell these fellows to do other things,
Besides all that preaching and praying?
Well, listen, JC, there's things ought to be said,
And I might as well get on with the saying.
Didn't you tell them "don't judge your fellow man"
And "love ye one another"
And "not put your faith in worldly goods".
Well, you should see the goods that they got, brother!
They got great big buildings and works of art,
And millions of dollars in real estate,
They got no time to care about human beings,
They forgot what you told 'em, mate;
Things like, "Whatever ye do to the least of my brothers,

This ye do also unto me".
Yeah, well these people who are using your good name,
They're abusing it, JC,
But there's people still living the way you lived,
And still copping the hypocrisy, racism and hate,
Getting crucified by the fat cats, too,
But they don't call us religious, mate.
Tho' we got the same basic values that you lived by,
Sharin' and carin' about each other,
And the bread and the wine that you passed around,
Well, we're still doing that, brother.
Yeah, we share our food and drink and shelter,
Our grief, our happiness, our hopes and plans,
But they don't call us "Followers of Jesus",
They call us black fellas, man.
But if you're still offering your hand in forgiveness
To the one who's done wrong, and is sorry,
I reckon we'll meet up later on,
And I got no cause to worry.
Just don't seem right somehow that all the good you did,
That people preach, not practise, what you said,
I wonder, if it all died with you, that day on the cross,
And if it just never got raised from the dead.

Good question from Maureen Watson.

Robert Walker is yet another young man who spent all his life looking for —he's a South Australian poet, or was—looking for his Mum and when he could not find his Mum he made up this big story and told the South Australian people that he was my third child—I'd had two children — and that I'd rejected him and handed him over to a white family to rear.

I couldn't imagine doing that. He just had to have a mother, so OK I was a fill-in, and finally I think everybody believed that he was my son and everywhere I went in Adelaide they'd say "How come you rejected your third son?"

I said "Darling, I only had two sons, that one is not mine, but if he needs a mother then I'll gladly fill in for him." Well he never did find his mother and now he's one of the statistics of the deaths in custody. One night he was in jail and he found a sock and he was with us no more. This is his poem called "Solitary Confinement":

> Have you ever been ordered to strip
> Before half a dozen barking eyes,
> Forcing you against a wall—
> Ordering you to part your legs and bend over?
>
> Have you ever had a door slammed
> Locking you out of the world,
> Propelling you into timeless space—
> To the emptiness of silence?
>
> Have you ever laid on a wooden bed—
> In regulation pyjamas,
> And tried to get a bucket to talk—
> In all seriousness?
>
> Have you ever begged for blankets
> From an eye staring through a hole in the door,
> Rubbing at the cold air digging into your flesh—
> Biting down on your bottom lip, while mouthing "Please, Sir"?
>
> Have you ever heard screams in the middle of the night,
> Or the sobbings of a stir-crazy prisoner,
> Echo over and over again in the darkness—
> Threatening to draw you into its madness?
>
> Have you ever rolled up into a human ball
> And prayed for sleep to come?

Have you ever laid awake for hours
Waiting for morning to mark yet another day of being alone?

If you've ever experienced even one of these,
Then bow your head and thank God.
For it's a strange thing indeed—
This rehabilitation system!

And to finish I'd like to say my poem because when I first started writing poetry, first of all they said "She's not writing this you know. A well-known Communist is writing it for her." That was when the good old Red Bogey was running about the streets and under the beds and everywhere. And then when they said "She must be writing these poems", they said "Well, the reason why she writes good poems is because she's not a full-blood, you know. She's got white man's blood in her, it's the white man's blood coming out in her." Then after a while they got a bit worried about me and they would say "Who is this woman? What is she trying to do to us? What is she up to? What kind of woman is she?" So I wrote "The Past" to tell everyone in the world who I am, what I am and why I am what I am. ["The Past", which Oodgeroo read here, is printed on p.159.] And when you think of the hundred thousand years of my people, and compare it to 205 years of the invaders, that 205 years is but a blink of an eyelash!

And in conclusion I'd like to say the Australian field of literature is vibrant, it's healthy and it's exciting. Australian writers can take their place with pride in the world literature field. I feel indeed humble and proud to be but a small part of such distinguished creative artists.

To the new Australians now taking their place in the Australian literature fields, to them I say "Welcome, welcome, welcome". May all their hands and minds continue with strength to grow. May the ink in their pens continue to flow.

Endnotes

BEGINNINGS

1 Quoted by James Devaney in the Foreword to Kath Walker, *We Are Going* (Brisbane: Jacaranda Press, 1964).

2 A.H. Campbell, L. Cameron, J.A. Keats, M.W. Poulter, B. Poulter, *The Aborigines and Torres Islanders of Queensland* (Brisbane: The Western Suburbs Branch of the United Nations Association, Brisbane, 1958).

3 The relevant acts were *The Aborigines Preservation and Protection Acts, 1939 - 1946* and *The Torres Strait Islanders Act, 1939.*

LEAVING HOME

1 John Collins, "A Mate in Publishing" in Adam Shoemaker, ed., *Oodgeroo and Her People: Perspectives on Her Life's Work*, (UQP: St Lucia, in publication).

MEETINGS

1 It seems that the Rev. Sweet later greatly changed his views. He became sincerely involved with the efforts of the Aurukun people to develop their own outstations and other social structures – efforts which were frustrated by the Queensland govenment of the day.

2 These provisions are as detailed in Campbell et al., *The Aborigines and Torres Islanders of Queensland* (Brisbane: The Western Suburbs Branch of the United Nations Association, Brisbane, 1958).

3 Oodgeroo, typescript held in the Kath Walker Collection, Fryer Library, University of Queensland.

RELATIONS

1 Extract from *Stradbroke Dreamtime* by Oodgeroo, illustrated by Bronwyn Bancroft (Sydney: Angus & Robertson, 1993).

2 This account is based on a typescript held in the Kath Walker collection, Fryer Library, University of Queensland.

3 Quoted in Terry Lane, *As the Twig Is Bent* (Melbourne: Dove Communications, 1979).

4 Extract from *Stradbroke Dreamtime* by Oodgeroo.

5 *Wynnum Herald*, 5 August 1964.

PROTEST!

1 Faith Bandler, *Wacvie* (Adelaide: Rigby, 1977).

2 Ex-boxer Ellie Bennett was sent to Palm Island when he was no longer boxing and was found drinking.

3 From Oodgeroo and Kabul, speech delivered at Griffith University, 1989, and printed in Oodgeroo, *My People* (Brisbane: Jacaranda, 1990, third edition).

4 *Australian*, 27 March 1969.

5 Kath Walker, "Coalition of Black and White Australians", unpublished paper written for circulation among members of FCAATSI before the Easter conference of 1970. (Communicated by A.B. Pittock)

6 Barrie Pittock, "A Personal View: Easter 1970 and the Origins of the National Tribal Council", in the Reports of the Brisbane Aboriginal and Islanders' Tribal Council, July–August 1970. (Communicated by A.B. Pittock)

7 Kath Walker, "Coalition of Black and White Australians."

MOONGALBA

1 Extract from *Stradbroke Dreamtime* by Oodgeroo, illustrated by Bronwyn Bancroft (Sydney: Angus & Robertson, 1993).

2 Ibid.

3 Judith Wright, *Born of the Conquerors* (Canberra: Aboriginal Studies Press, 1991).

4 Kath Walker, typescript held in the Kath Walker Collection, Fryer Library, University of Queensland.

5 Ibid.

6 H.C. Coombs, *ABC Guest of Honour Address* reported in Stewart Harris, *It's Coming Yet…* (Canberra: The Aboriginal Treaty Committee, 1979).

7 Judith Wright, *Born of the Conquerors*.

8 Kath Walker and Julianne Schwenke, Submission to the Federal Government Department of Aboriginal Affairs, 1979. Copy held in the Kath Walker Collection, Fryer Library, University of Queensland.

9 Judith Wright, *Born of the Conquerors*.

10 Extract from *Stradbroke Dreamtime* by Oodgeroo.

11 Margaret Read Lauer, "Kath Walker at Moongalba: Making a New Dreamtime" in *World Literature Written in English* 17:1 (April 1978).

12 *Courier-Mail*, 14 October 1983.

13 Kath Walker and Julianne Schwenke, Submission, 1979.

ACCLAIM

1 The following account is based on a paper by Kath Walker entitled *Flight Into Tunis*, dated 14 December 1974, held in the Kath Walker collection, Fryer Library, University of Queensland.

2 Text held in the Kath Walker Collection, Fryer Library, University of Queensland.

3 Kath Walker, speech delivered at the Australian National University, Canberra, in 1979 and reprinted in *My People* (Brisbane: Jacaranda, 1981, second edition).

4 John Collins, "A Mate in Publishing" in Adam Shoemaker, ed., Oodgeroo and Her People: Perspectives on Her Life's Work (St Lucia: UQP, in publication).

5 Manning Clark, Introduction to *Kath Walker in China* (Brisbane: Jacaranda Press and International Culture Publishing Corporation, 1988).

6 John Collins, "A Mate in Publishing".

7 Kath Walker, *The Dawn Is At Hand: Poems* (London: Marion Boyars, 1992).

OODGEROO

1 Robert Hughes, *The Fatal Shore* (London: Collins Harvill, 1987).

2 Ibid.

3 Oodgeroo and Kabul, speech delivered at Griffith University, 1989, printed in Oodgeroo, *My People* (Brisbane: Jacaranda, 1990, third edition).

4 John Collins, "A Mate in Publishing" in Adam Shoemaker, ed., *Oodgeroo and Her People: Perspectives on Her Life's Work* (St Lucia: UQP, in publication).

5 Extract from *Stradbroke Dreamtime* by Oodgeroo, illustrated by Bronwyn Bancroft (Sydney: Angus & Robertson, 1993).

6 Quoted in Stewart Harris, *It's Coming Yet…* (Canberra: The Aboriginal Treaty Committee, 1979).

7 Stewart Harris, *It's Coming Yet…*

8 This quotation and those that follow concerning production of *The Rainbow Serpent* are by Ann Derham, in a personal communication with the author.

9 Oodgeroo and Kabul, *The Rainbow Serpent* (Canberra: AGPS, 1988).

10 Ibid.

11 Peter Knudtson and David Suzuki, *Wisdom of the Elders* (Toronto: Stoddart Publishing Company, 1992).

THIS LITTLE NOW

1 Extract from *Stradbroke Dreamtime* by Oodgeroo, illustrated by Bronwyn Bancroft (Sydney: Angus & Robertson, 1993).

2 North Stradbroke Island Housing Co-operative, *Strategic Development Plan, 1991 to 1992* (Dunwich, 1990).

3 Ibid.

4 John Collins, "Oodgeroo of the Tribe Noonuccal", *Race and Class* 35:4 (April-June) 1994.

5 Judith Wright, "Landscape and Dreaming" in Stephen Graubard, ed., *Australia – The Daedalus Symposium* (North Ryde: Angus & Robertson, 1985).

THE POETRY

1 For the "assimilation doctrine" see, for example, Tigger Wise, *The Self-Made Anthropologist: A Life of A.P. Elkin* (Sydney: George Allen and Unwin, 1985), esp. pp. 228–30.

2 James Press, *Rule and Energy: Trends in British Poetry Since the Second World War* (Oxford: Oxford University Press, 1963).

3 Adam Shoemaker, *Black Words, White Page: Aboriginal Literature 1929-1988* (St Lucia: University of Queensland Press, 1989).

List of Copyright Holders

The author acknowledges the following publishers and individuals for their permission to reprint copyright material:

Angus & Robertson for "Mirrabooka", "Paperbark Tree", and extracts from "Dugong Coming!" (including "Myora…", p. 89), "Kill to Eat", "Burr-Nong" and "Carpet Snake", from *Stradbroke Dreamtime* by Oodgeroo, illustrated by Bronwyn Bancroft (1993); for the poems, "Eroded Hills", "Old House", "Bora Ring" and "Canefields", by Judith Wright from her *Collected Poems* and "Two Dreamtimes" from *A Human Pattern* by Judith Wright.

Jacaranda Wiley for the poems by Oodgeroo, "A Song of Hope", "Aboriginal Charter of Rights", "Artist Son", "Assimilation—No!", "Civilisation", "Colour Bar", "Cookalingee" , "Gooboora, the Silent Pool", "Integration—Yes!", "Oh Trugganner!", "Reed Flute Cave", "Son of Mine", "The Past", "The Teachers", "We Are Going", "Whynot Street" and for the prose by Oodgeroo and Kabul "Custodians of the Land" from *My People* by Oodgeroo (1990, third edition); and for "Tienanmen Square" and "Requiem" from *Kath Walker in China* by Oodgeroo (with International Culture Publishing Corporation, 1988).

Jack Davis for "First Born" from *The First Born and Other Poems* (J.M. Dent, 1983); Mudrooroo for "They Give Jacky Rights" from *The Song Circle of Jacky and Selected Poems* (Hyland House, 1986); Lyndall Ryan for extracts from her unpublished PhD thesis on the Aborigines of Tasmania, Macquarie University, c. 1976. Charlotte Walker for "Solitary Confinement" by Robert Walker.

Denis Walker and Petrina Walker for *The Rainbow Serpent* by Oodgeroo and Kabul; Maureen Watson for "Stepping Out" and "Memo to JC".

Acknowledgment is also made to individuals and organisations who provided photographs: BTQ 7 (pp. 114, 115); George Fetting (cover, p. 2); Fryer Memorial Library (pp. 14, 16, 26, 36, 38 [group], 59, 62, 71, 83); Queensland State and Municipal Choir (p. 124); *Redland Times* (pp. 104, 142, 156, 157, 158); and Brian Clouston, John Collins, Carolyn Davis, Patricia Walker and Petrina Walker who lent photographs from private collections.

Every effort has been made to trace copyright holders, but in a few cases this has proved impossible. The publishers would be interested to hear from any copyright holders not here acknowledged.